SpringerBriefs in B

MW01246083

For further volumes:
http://www.springer.com/series/8860

Alan L. Carsrud · Malin Brännback

Family Firms in Transition

Case Studies on Succession, Inheritance, and Governance

 Springer

Alan L. Carsrud
Ted Rogers School of Management
Ryerson University
Toronto, Ontario, Canada
alan.carsrud@ryerson.ca

Malin Brännback
School of Business and Economics
Åbo Akademi University
Turku, Finland
malin.brannback@abo.fi

ISSN 2191-5482   e-ISSN 2191-5490
ISBN 978-1-4614-1200-7   e-ISBN 978-1-4614-1201-4
DOI 10.1007/978-1-4614-1201-4
Springer New York Dordrecht Heidelberg London

Library of Congress Control Number: 2011937052

Springer is part of Springer Science+Business Media (www.springer.com)

Acknowledgments

We are grateful to the Price Center for Entrepreneurial Studies in the Anderson School at UCLA for their support in the early development of some of the cases in this volume and to the Ewing Marion Kauffman Foundation of Kansas City, MO for their support of the development of those cases developed at Florida International University. Without our students at the University of California, Los Angeles, Florida International University, Ryerson University, Pepperdine University, and Åbo Akademi University it would have been impossible to bring these cases to life and to make these stories available to a wider audience.

Contents

Chapter 1
Introduction

In this series of cases on family owned and managed business, we focus on the governance of the firm and family and how governance, or lack thereof, impacts succession of leadership in the firm and the inheritance of ownership and wealth. We have clustered these topics together because the social systems of the family and the management system of the firm have significant impacts on the success, or failure, of succession plans. We believe that all the planning in the world for succession and inheritance will not succeed if the firm does not have a well established and functional governance system. Likewise, if the family does not understand its role in the governance of the firm and the mechanisms for making a decision within the firm, succession choices may not be accepted by family members. Most family firms fail because of succession issues, not economic ones.

It is the role of governance and how it impacts both family and firm that link these family business cases together with succession and inheritance. Succession can also be seen as part of the changes facing the firm over time. What to do is never clear and often not obvious. One must remember that dealing with succession and inheritance are fraught with uncertainty. The best laid plans can and do go astray. While the cases in this book initially were developed as a part of the curriculum for teaching family business to both graduate and undergraduate business school students in the United States, Canada, Australia, and Finland. However, we feel their utility goes beyond the classroom and should be informative to consultants to family firms and family business owners as well. Often reading about the issues others have faced and how they have dealt with these can provide clarity to one's own issues.

The purpose of a case in family business is not to expound on one correct answer to a particular problem. What a case does do is to show the relative complexity of issues facing family firms that depend on a number of players coming to some agreement to a solution that works for all concerned. Sometimes this is successfully done, in other cases the resolution to a problem is less than ideal. We believe strongly that cases on succession and governance allows others in family business to see they too are not alone in dealing with similar issues. Cases can provide those in a family firm with a chance to see how different scenarios can play out within the complex fabric of a family owned and managed firm.

A.L. Carsrud and M. Brännback, *Family Firms in Transition: Case Studies on Succession, Inheritance, and Governance*, SpringerBriefs in Business 3, DOI 10.1007/978-1-4614-1201-4_1, © Alan L. Carsrud and Malin Brännback, 2011

Many of the cases in this book have been de-identified. In others, the cases are on real firms but using only information available to the general public. In few cases, the names have not been changed as the family has agreed to let their information be public in the hopes it will assist other family firms. We hope that by reading these cases, both families in business and students will come to appreciate the issues faced by family firms and the complexity of the systems (family, management, and ownership) that interact to influence the decisions made concerning the firm.

While some of these cases may discuss events in the past, the issues are as relevant today as they were the day they were first faced by the individuals in the firm. Most of the cases are brief, less than 15 pages in length. They are not meant to be a complete representation of the family, the firm, or the situation. They are meant, however, to give the reader a feeling for what is being faced in the cases and the people in the case who are going to have to make some decisions with respect to handling succession and inheritance.

Each case in this volume contains some history of the firm. Information is provided on the relevant family members. Some cases have important nonfamily employees who are also described in the case. Many cases are written from the perspective of a protagonist who is looking upon the situation and trying to decide what to do. As the reader you may, or may not, wish to put yourself in the place of that protagonist.

Children, Succession, and Governance

Succession in family owned and managed businesses, as well as public companies has been widely studies by scholars and consultants for decades. While the academic research has applied different theoretical approaches and data, the complexity of the phenomena remains best demonstrated by the written case. It is through the case that we can see how different perspectives can be applied, sometimes simultaneously. For example, the strategic management literature has investigated succession by adopting a perspective of "upper echelons" where the selection of a new CEO is a decision that impacts the future direction of the business, and to some degree the family who owns the firm. This literature focuses on the performance outcomes of succession, successor type, post-succession conflict, and founder/successor characteristics. Succession is one of the leading topics studied by family business academics. The family business literature has focused on qualitative aspects of succession, such as the succession process, the role of the founder, the perspectives of the next generation and the characteristics of effective successions.

Despite research from a number of perspectives, succession research is far from being conclusive. The relationship between succession and firm performance is mixed in the majority of cases. We conclude from that fact that succession is largely dependent upon the specific contexts in which it occurs and is often dependent on the unique players involved. We also argue that family businesses represent a context in which succession has a special meaning as it may mean both leader of the firm and leader of the family. There are two reasons for this, in family firms being a part of the family with all its relationships is very different from being an outsider. Being a part of the "in group of the family" can and does influence the succession outcome. In addition, the overlaps between managerial, ownership, and family positions in family owned and managed businesses makes succession particularly traumatic, especially when the CEO is the founder of the firm, the head of the family, and the primary owner of the firm.

Family firms have characteristics that have been referred to the "familiness" of the firm. One can think of these as set of unique resources created by the interaction of the family and their firm. However, these resources must be activated and used. Many of these assets are contained within the tacit collective knowledge embedded in the firm. Their importance becomes obvious when there is a transfer of this tacit knowledge through a successful succession and thus contributes to a sustainable competitive advantage. Research shows that tacit knowledge is one of the factors that can make an intergenerational succession the preferred transfer of leadership.

Managers of publicly held firms often use sophisticated systems for managerial control, including formal corporate governance mechanisms. These are employed to ensure successful and sustainable performance of the firm, show transparency, and gain trust from the company's shareholders and the investment community. However, family businesses show less commitment to formal mechanisms for governance of either the firm or the family. This reluctance can impact success of the firm and a successful succession of CEO leadership. This reluctance may be the result of seeing greater benefits from nonfinancial goals then financial goals, thus feeling there is less need for the optimization of financial performance of the firm where accountability is easier to measure. In family firms, decision-making is often based on intuition and experience rather than operating figures. But, it also must be recognized that often founders of family firms are reluctant to share information on performance with family stakeholders and this results in an aversion to dedicate resources to a control systems and governance. However, family firms may install proper governance and management control systems to oversee non-family managers and meet the information requirements by banks and nonmanagement family members who are owners.

Chapter 2
Reading a Family Business Case

In reading a family business case you will see the unique issues faced by entrepreneurs and their family firms. To get the most from these cases you should ask yourself the following questions:

- What is the situational context of the case?
- Who are the principal players?
- Who do I identify within the case?
- What are the pertinent facts in case?
- Have I looked closely at the exhibits?
- What concepts about family business and management in general should apply to this case?
- Does this case represent a situation that I might face?

Reading a family business case should help you, the reader, to understand key concepts through self-discovery. In this process you will learn that there is no permanent right answer for any family business situation and that there are many different ways to handle issues facing a family firm. We hope we have developed a series of cases that will have compelling situations so interesting questions can be asked. You will find these at the end of each case under the heading, "Learning Notes."

Our goal is to help you to ask penetrating questions about how you would have handled the situation if you had been involved in this situation. This should help you learn different courses of action, perhaps find a better to solve a situation in the case. However, please remember that business cases are often messy and confusing. But, family business cases are even more "messy" just like families themselves. You will discover that firm problems are rarely found in neatly wrapped packages.

When reading a case please remember that they are not histories, but often are built in historic fashion. They clearly are stories of a family and their firm and thus are a part of the narrative tradition so much a part of all cultures. We have edited them to reduce the level of "noise of everyday life" but they do represent a selection of facts and inferences that, we believe, presents a learning situation. We have done

A.L. Carsrud and M. Brännback, *Family Firms in Transition: Case Studies on Succession, Inheritance, and Governance*, SpringerBriefs in Business 3, DOI 10.1007/978-1-4614-1201-4_2, © Alan L. Carsrud and Malin Brännback, 2011

this to allow the reader to step into the situation/opportunity being faced by someone else. We hope we have created a microcosm of life of a business-owning family and of the life within their family firm.

About Cases

Case are developed by the research team and authors so that the reader has to respond to a situation where there is some form of action required. Often there are a range of possible actions available, which require applying a range of different skills. They are usually written from the standpoint of someone in the case who is the protagonist. While families and firms are highly complex, the writing team, for purposes of clarity, picked a limited set of foci for the situation within the family and firm. Often this is influenced by the current research literature in the field which can be applied to the case. As much as possible, this review of the literature helps create an outline of the situation providing a basis for the logical flow of case facts. The authors try to communicate the action of the case in a engaging manner, providing relevant facts and not overloading the case with irrelevant material. You will find in cases things like biographical sketches of players along with financial data, industry information, or other information believed to be critical for understanding the case. In the end, we are hoping to tell a story where there may or may not be an obvious solution to the problem. All of these cases are based on real people and we hope that their humanity comes through in what has been written.

There are four basic case styles: (1) Highly Structured Cases; (2) Short Vignettes; (3) Long Unstructured Cases; and (4) Ground Breaking Cases. We will briefly review each of these so you can appreciate the variety of the cases provided.

The *Highly Structured Case* is typically short, contains no excess information, its problem is well-ordered and stated. In such a case there exists a best solution. One can apply known tools or models and within the case there is sufficient data available for solution to be derived. Several of the cases in this series of case books fall within this category.

Another variety of cases are those best described as *Short Vignettes*. These are typically used to introduce a key concept, such as succession planning. They typically offer little excess information. They may be rather short, from 1 to 10 pages. What may be surprising in these types of cases is that the best answer is *not* derived from simple formula. These types of cases are usually used as a short teaching vehicle to get across one or two concepts. Some of the cases in this series fall into this category, but as with all family business cases, complexity usually is the dominant feature.

The next form is the *Long Unstructured Case*. It is typically 10–50 pages, often with several exhibits including financial data and industrial sector commentary. These longer cases are when the writers want to reflect the reality of a situation with more of its complexity. This is done by providing nearly all needed information about situation. Because these cases are full of both qualitative and quantitative information it is often more difficult to apply financial models to the problem. This is because the underlying problems and/or opportunities facing the firm and family are unclear. These cases do cover terrain where knowledge exists and/or there are preferred practices about how family issues can be address. It is these types of cases that should lead the reader to want to explore the existing research literature in family business, entrepreneurship, and general management. There are examples of this type of case in this series of case studies. You will find exhibits in these cases such as financial statements, organizational diagrams, etc. Many times these exhibits are unique or specific to the family business case and some of these may be "uncommon" or surprising.

The final type is known as the *Ground Breaking Case*. They are usually written by and for advanced MBA and doctoral students. This allows students and instructor engaged in joint exploration. From a research standpoint these are usually the first stage in looking at an under research phenomena where little existing or prior knowledge exists on which to base systematic research. These are the cases which have as a goal extending the knowledge base. While it would have been nice to put such a case into this series, these frankly end up as books unto themselves or become doctoral dissertations.

Learning Notes

At the end of each case you will find a *Learning Notes*. These are typically directed to faculty members to use to direct class discussion, if they are using the case in an educational setting. In these volumes, we direct these to the reader as questions the reader should be asking themselves. In some cases the concepts may be tied to the existing research literature when possible. Sometimes these notes state the obvious focus of this case. At other times they may also discuss the hidden issues in the case. Hopefully they will challenge the reader to think about what business skills, or knowledge, they should apply to case.

Chapter 3
Case One: The Packard Marketing Group – Letting Children into the Business

This case was developed by Randy Dorilag and Julie Khoe and written under the supervision of Alan Carsrud. The case is an example of how children often enter a parent's business. This case does not provide a solution, but rather tells the story of how intentions of parents concerning children in the firm and how intentions of children about being in the firm can ultimately affect the family firm. The names in this case have been changed, but the content is totally factual.

Introduction

It was a warm and sunny April morning, and Nancy Packard sat in her Los Angeles office wondering what to do next. As president of the Packard Marketing Group ("PMG"), she needed to recruit an employee who could both assume her duties as creative manager, and work well with her son, Steven Packard. Steven had been a critical factor behind the departure of a talented senior employee, and would undoubtedly have trouble working with many of the potential candidates that Nancy was considering. Stephan headed the firm's business development, marketing services, and financial functions. Firing her son was not an option; Stephan had managed to grow the firm rapidly while he reduced costs, making the firm profitable. Nancy wondered how she found herself in this complex situation, especially since she had pledged never to involve family members in PMG's operations. When she thought back over the past decade, Nancy was able to identify three key periods in PMG's history: founding the business, relinquishing responsibility for the firm's day-to-day operations when she moved to New York, and finally, hiring her son and positioning the firm for growth.

A.L. Carsrud and M. Brännback, *Family Firms in Transition: Case Studies on Succession,*
Inheritance, and Governance, SpringerBriefs in Business 3,
DOI 10.1007/978-1-4614-1201-4_3, © Alan L. Carsrud and Malin Brännback, 2011

The Early Years

First there was the merger of Nancy's former employer, The Brownlee Company, with another large public relations firm presented Nancy and fellow employee, Paul Swartz, with an opportunity. They decided to form their own public relations firm, taking with them one client who did not want to remain with the newly merged firm. Nancy had always relished the idea of practicing creative public relations without the bureaucratic hassles of a large firm. She could easily afford the risk, as her husband's successful career as a law professor provided the family with ample income and Nancy with a great degree of freedom.

Initially, the two founders focused on having fun rather than making profits. Nancy treated the business as a hobby, which was reflected in her interest in handling existing accounts rather than building the business. Her partner, Paul, also "dabbled at the business" – he worked short hours and did not contribute much to the firm's growth. The firm's survival was based on Nancy's success at retaining current clients and, ironically, in attracting new clients who knew her through former business encounters.

When founding the business, Nancy pledged to her partner, and to her husband, to limit family involvement. She had a verbal agreement with her son Greg, who worked for another public relations firm that they would not work together. Her other son Steven, had never shown an interest in marketing and public relations. Thus, Nancy never thought that he would ask to enter the business. Her husband was the only family member interested in any part of the operations; he served as a sounding board for Nancy, personally reviewing any proposals before they were submitted to clients.

After 2 years of watching Paul develop no new business, Nancy decided to purchase his interest in PMG, thus taking complete control. Without Paul, Nancy needed to find someone committed to helping her run the company. She hired a nonfamily member, Melody Webber, to serve as her "right hand." Melody quickly showed an instinct for the business and soon became the agency's first account executive. Soon afterwards, an assistant was hired for Melody. For the first time, the firm began to grow.

Making a Family Decision: Moving to New York

Just over a year after Melody had joined the firm, Nancy's husband, David, a law professor at UCLA, received a distinguished joint professorship at Yale University and New York University. At this time, Nancy made two decisions: a *family* decision to accompany her husband, and a corresponding *business* decision to leave the daily office responsibilities, temporarily, with Melody, her trusted and newly promoted account executive.

While in New York, Nancy continued to conduct business. She would speak with Melody via telephone several times each day to maintain internal communications. The internet made working remotely much easier. Additionally, Nancy would return to the office approximately 1 week/month to personally meet with Melody and the agency's clients. Nancy and Melody mastered these arrangements so that clients never knew that Nancy was conducting business physically from New York.

In order to allow Melody to concentrate on the creative side of the business, Nancy hired an external firm to take care of the agency's operational and administrative issues. In Nancy's eyes, this arrangement seemed ideal: the outside firm subleased adjacent office space, and was able to keep a close watch on the business. Nancy later learned, however, that in her absence, this arrangement brought significant financial problems to PMG.

A Son Enters the Business

Nancy was completely unprepared when Steven, her son, called her in New York and asked her if he could join the firm. He had graduated from Berkeley with a business degree and after 2 years in an international banking position in San Francisco, decided being in the family firm was a better career option. Nancy reacted by saying to a close friend "What on earth will you do?" He had never worked in public relations, his education was not in a relevant discipline, and there was hardly enough business to justify a full-time employee to handle the firm's finances. Moreover, she already had a great account executive.

After much discussion, Nancy stood by her initial decision and refused to blindly create an unneeded position for her son. However, Nancy, not wanting to tell her son "no" so directly, thought that she would apply a "business like approach" to getting Steven to remove himself from being in the firm. Nancy asked Steven to draft a job description and business plan which would detail his new role in the company. She frankly never thought he would take the time to give her such a document. As she looked back, Nancy regretted that she had not created her own plan, clearly outlining not only her son's function, but hers. What he had not done well was outline how his position worked with that of Melody's.

Nevertheless, Steven's plan was creative and thorough. He created job descriptions for almost everyone, including a job entitled "director of operations and business development." This position handled all administrative functions, thereby reducing the time that Nancy spent on "unbillable" paperwork, and eliminating the need for the agent. In addition, Stephan tasked himself with generating marketing campaigns aimed at the development of new business. The plan called for aggressive growth, which would enable the firm to hire additional personnel and provide careers for her son and others.

Nancy was impressed with the thoroughness of the plan and could hardly say "no" to her own son who had shown great initiative in build an overall plan for the business. Evidently the faculty at Berkeley had taught him well in his business planning class. Only now did Nancy understand the shortcomings of her challenge to her son. Not only did the plan change the thrust of the agency from that of a hobby business to a serious professional firm, but the plan also failed to provide clear guidelines for Melody's future. Nancy felt forced to give her son a position as he had done what she asked, and done it well.

The Success and Failures of Hiring a Child

Within 3 years, Steven accomplished many tasks. His business development efforts brought many new clients to the firm. In addition, he undertook a review of PMG's financial situation. During this time Stephan fired the external agent after discovering that they had not been paying the company's bills. Shortly thereafter, Steven established an accounts payable system and cleared the company's bad debts within the first 6 months.

While he had many successes, Steven's entrance also created a difficult situation for Melody. Although Nancy had always valued both Melody's hard work and friendship, Nancy still permitted Steven to assume an authoritative "caretaker" role while she was in New York. As a result, Steven often criticized Melody's work with PMG's clients, citing a lack of professionalism. Understandably, Melody did not accept his criticisms graciously, for she had grown accustomed to being her own boss. In addition, the fact that Steven was fairly inexperienced in business led Melody, an experienced and older employee, to question many of Steven's suggestions.

In Nancy's absence, Steven and Nancy each developed their own ideas about their office responsibilities. Steven immediately took responsibility for evaluating and making corrections to PMG's operations. These changes occurred on both the financial side, which was clearly his responsibility, and on the creative side, which overlapped with Melody's job function. Steven felt that his recommendations to Melody were justified because he was acting in the best interests of his family's business. However, Melody felt that Steven was interfering with her work and constantly thwarting the independence that Nancy had granted her previously. The age and gender differences between the two further complicated the already tense situation.

To make matters worse, Melody was uncertain as to her future role in the company. As an outsider and without any communication from Nancy, Melody began to doubt if she had a future at PMG, even though both Stephan and Nancy viewed her as an essential asset of the firm. Within a year of Steven's arrival Melody could no longer handle the tensions between Steven and herself and as a result, she resigned.

Current Situation

Melody's exit prompted PMG to hire a new account manager, John Ellison. While John had the experience required to handle many of the account management functions performed by Melody, he lacked her creative talents. Steven moved quickly to fill the gap, assuming the role of Nancy's right hand man, and even taking on the creative tasks of the firm's projects. Clearly, this did not sit too well with John. Within a year of Steven's arrival the firm had seven employees and clients across the country, not just in southern California.

While some of Steven's decisions enhanced his relationships with employees, others backfired. Early on, Steven assumed responsibilities for running PMG's day-to-day operations. To bolster employee relations, Steven took it upon himself to close the office early on Friday afternoons when the workload permitted. Understandably, the staff did not object, and moreover, they presumed that Steven had the authority to make this decision. Stephan had not notified his mother about this practice. On the other hand, Steven felt that it was his duty to report to his mother any situations or employee actions which might have been detrimental to PMG. While his intentions were honorable, most of the employees viewed Steven suspiciously because of this reporting arrangement.

Steven received several other privileges. He took extra days off with pay, did not receive standard performance reviews, collected new business commissions over the life of the project rather than for the standard 6 month period, and questioned Nancy's decisions and strategies. Although the quality of Steven's work made these privileges well deserved, the fact remained that a nonfamily member had not been given such liberties. Nancy wondered if this "ad hoc" treatment would become an issue as the firm grew larger.

If PMG were to continue to grow, key employees such as John Ellison, would have to feel comfortable with the implied authority which came with Steven's status as the "boss' son." Obviously, not every employee could accept this reality, as evidenced by Melody's departure earlier. Despite the problems created by Steven's special treatment, Nancy increasingly felt that his presence was essential to the livelihood of the agency. He had been a key factor in generating new business for the firm, and possessed the business skills which many creative types lacked. Nancy found the thought of terminating her own son extremely difficult to conceive. However, she admitted that if another employee had made the same mistakes and had caused PMG such considerable headaches, the nonfamily employee would have been fired. While Steven felt that he was not necessarily immune from dismissal, he knew that it would be difficult for his mother to fire him.

Future Possibilities

Nancy had already endorsed PMG's plans to grow from 8 to 15 employees within the next 5 years – given the increase in client development – and realized that staffing increases were essential in order to maintain the health of the firm. Yet she fears what might happen, particularly if she had to leave town once again to follow her husband on an overseas assignment. Nancy knew additional creative talent needed to be hired if she were to limit her involvement with accounts. But how could she find a person with both the creative skills needed to grow PMG's accounts and the management skills required to keep her son in check?

Nancy saw that several options existed, each with its own problems. She could fire Steven and hire a replacement, but this choice would ruin her family relations which were much more important to her than the business. Another option was to attempt to hire Steven's brother, but she knew that the two rarely got along; their relationship was cordial at best and the potential increase in the tension level at work would likely encourage further resignations among the remaining staff members. She could even attempt to reassert her presence in the firm in an effort to control her son's self-indulgent management style which can promote employee morale, but wondered if it was too late to do so. Nancy's next move was unclear, but she realized that she had to act quickly.

Learning Notes

In this case, the reader can see how family sometimes enters a business even when the intention of the founder is to not have family involved. This is also an example of how intentions of children concerning their role in their parent's business change over time and how these shifts can ultimately impact not only the growth and direction of the firm, but ultimately the succession of leadership within the firm. This case does not provide an outcome to the dilemma but it should challenge the reader to think about what they would have done differently in Nancy's situation, if anything.

Chapter 4
Case Two: Gazi Family Constitution – Managing the Family in a Family Firm

Introduction

This is less a case in the traditional sense as it is an example of the outcome of one of the Turkish family business creating a mechanism for the governance of the family members with respect to the family business. This constitution has been "de-identified" in terms of names and firm. It does represent how a modern secular Turkish family has addressed the need to assure a stable set of family values with respect to their business. As such within this constitution they have set out to define terms, state a history of the business, and to define the rights and responsibilities of family members, vis-à-vis the firm. The wording of the constitution is that of the family who drafted it first in Turkish and then translated it into English. The only changes were to names and locations.

The Constitution

This Constitution encompasses the relations (monetary, financial, legal) among the current and future offspring of Mr. Argun Gazi, and the businesses and organizations (both profit and nonprofit) founded by Argun Gazi and Ece Gazi.

Definitions

1. Celil Gazi: First Generation
2. Argun Gazi, Ece Gazi: Second Generation
3. Ful Cagatay, Lale Saatchi, and Emine Gazi Fehime: Third Generation
4. Argun Gazi and Ece Gazi, and their offspring Ful Cagatay, Lale Saatchi, and Emine Gazi Bazar: Founders of the Constitution

A.L. Carsrud and M. Brännback, *Family Firms in Transition: Case Studies on Succession, Inheritance, and Governance*, SpringerBriefs in Business 3, DOI 10.1007/978-1-4614-1201-4_4, © Alan L. Carsrud and Malin Brännback, 2011

5. Offspring of Ful Cagatay, Lale Saatchi, Emine Gazi Bazar (in order of age):
   Deha Saatchi, Yagiz Cagatay, Kaan Cagatay, Burcu Fehime, Baki Fehime and
   their spouses: Fourth Generation
6. The offspring of the Fourth Generation: Fifth and Sixth Generation, Seventh
   Generations, and so on
7. Currently established educational institutions from Kindergarten, through
   University: Schools and University
8. Eskisehir Educational Foundation (EEV): Foundation
9. Eskisehir Universitesi, of which the Foundation is the founder: University
10. EU Services Inc.; Eskisehir Construction Inc.; Eskisehir Publishing and Press
    Inc.; Eskisehir Education Services Inc.; and companies to be established later
    on: Companies
11. The whole sum of individuals identified as members of the Second Generation
    and beyond: Family
12. Council formed by the members of the family defined in the Constitution:
    Family Council

Explanations

Celil Gazi, identified as First Generation in this Constitution, established a private
teaching institution "Home of Learning" in the year 1928 in Izmir. He started one
of the first distance education programs in Turkey after he became an affiliate of
the German "Fenschule," a degree-by-mail organization that provided engineering
education. He later move his business to Eskisehir and continued his work in engineering education field until just before his death in 1960. Although this Constitution
identified Celil Gazi as the First Generation, his children other than Argun Gazi are
not subject to this Constitution.

Mission

Argun Gazi and his wife, Ece Gazi, founded a school, named Eskisehir Koleji, in
1960 following the death of Argun's father. In the ensuing years, growth has occurred
and their business is now a chain of educational institutions including kindergartens,
primary and secondary schools, and science high schools. These were established in
many locations in the western half of Turkey. In 1990, Eskisehir Universitesi was
added to the portfolio of educationally based services and schools. The university
has branches in Izmir, Ankara, and Istanbul as well as in Eskisehir. In addition,
the education-oriented businesses encompass many organizations, both profit and
nonprofit alike, which are active in diverse areas related to providing quality private
education in Turkey.

There was significant progress in the quality of the work performed, along with a progress in monetary, intellectual, financial, and real assets of the organizations. The number of students enrolled and the number of personnel employed has increased markedly throughout the years. The schools and the university have became a brand name in Turkey and the Middle East, as they reached thousands of student alumni, while hundreds of employees served them. Further improvements are envisioned.

Education work and its organization, its management have some very particular characteristics in an honoring profession, an honorable service provided to the country and families and the nation. These characteristics of the educational profession exalt the schools and institutions, along with their founders. As a result, making money remains a secondary objective in education and for this firm. Under all conditions; the proceeds from the businesses should be invested back into physical, academic, and technological facilities, for creating a conductive environment for modern, high-quality education.

The aim of this Constitution is to organize the relations among the different generations of family members, shareholders, and companies, schools and institutions in ways that would prevent conflicts in the management of schools, companies, and other institutions by ensuring the long-term continuity of values and principles set out by their founders and guiding in the formulation of solutions in case of possible disagreements.

History: Entry in Education

Argun Gazi received his higher education in the field of Civil Engineering at Middle East University in Ankara. During his six years of higher education, he lived in his father's teaching environment, working as a tutor in his father's private course center. For this reason, teaching was a part of his immediate environment. When in 1950 he became an engineer, he moved to the construction sector and left his father's business. Until 1959, he remained in the construction sector, which he had to leave after a 300% devaluation of the Turkish currency in 1958. While he went bankrupt, the central government decided to bail out the construction sector but by this time his father had closed his business and Argun and his wife decided to establish their own firm focused on private education in 1960. This was the first step in the private education sector. It was not a bad decision to quit the tense and cumbersome work of construction and go into education. He felt he knew the field having worked for his father's private education endeavors as a tutor. A lot of innovation could be done in the field of private education, and Argun Gazi carried these out in an exemplary fashion, for the other private schools and the national education establishment to appreciate and immolate.

Strategies for Establishing Success in Education

Private education was managed in the 1960s in a nonprofessional way. Argun Gazi had instructed students from such schools while working at his father's organization and seen that such schools were inadequate. When Eskisehir Koleji started operations it guaranteed its students, teachers, and parents an education that would be done with utmost respect for quality. Within a few years, Eskisehir Koleji was seen to be a special school, and attention from the public was mounting. Student numbers increased following investments in new and expanded facilities. These changes necessitated academic, physical, and managerial change and innovation. The most valuable teachers in the region were recruited. Educational matters such as discipline, methodology, and homework were elaborated. Testing and guidance offices were established. This was a first in Turkey. The Turkish Ministry of Education praised the school for its creative and innovative approaches in education and commented on the fact that many graduates were going to the best universities in Turkey and Europe. Modern management techniques were implemented for the growing school system. Hence, education and modern management principles worked alongside each other and Eskisehir Koleji.

We prioritized the new social and global realities and the expectations of Turkish families. This was our first principle of strategy. Second, we moved beyond purely educational principles. We viewed our schools as modern enterprises and managed them with the latest management knowledge of the new era. This knowledge relates to the establishment of the organization and carrying out the work, in addition to functions of finance; planning, budgeting, and managerial accounting.

Prioritized Values of the Family

Founder Argun Gazi has made it his duty to continue providing a high-quality education service despite the many ups and downs experienced in the Turkish economic, social, and political spheres. He wishes above all to see that education continues in the same manner in later generations in the family. This Constitution is written to ensure that the family retains its core values in successive generations.

In all of our schools, it should be our priority to cultivate individuals committees to the Ataturk's ideals who will uphold the nation's interest above his/her own interest. We will honor our modern and secular country founded by Ataturk. All executives, teachers, and faulty (from kindergarten to university) must be committed to these principles and should be removed in case they deviate from these principles. This clause should be included without qualifications and signed in their employment contracts. This is a fundamental principle prioritized by the family.

The family believes in the importance of the following its core values while dealing with its internal matters: In all relations within the family, openness and transparency should be the norm. Being tolerant and taking care to keep the interest if the

family and our institutions above their own interest or the interes
or children, is expected. Every generation should abide by these r
als should raise children in line with these principles.

Principle 1: Individuals shall be transparent in all relations \
  (*Principle of Openness*).

Principle 2: Individuals shall be tolerant in all relations within the family (*Principle of Tolerance*).

Principle 3: Individuals shall not put the interests of themselves, their spouses, or children ahead of the interests of the family and the institutions (*Principles of Conflict of Interest*).

Principle 4: Our institutions are labor-intensive organizations. Until today in all our organizations, we revered labor and did not treat employees unfairly. For this reason, the rights of labor should be sacred and should be kept this way in every generation (*Principle of Sacred Labor*).

Principle 5: All members of the family should possess the qualities of a good Turkish citizen and act with the rights and responsibilities associated with it (paying taxes, love of the motherland etc.) (*Principle of Sense of Citizenship*).

Principle 6: All members of the family should abide by the supremacy and rule of law, universal human rights, and ethical conduct (*Principle of the Supremacy and Rule of Law and Ethics*).

Responsibilities of the Family to Society

The responsibilities of the family members towards Turkish society are part of the responsibility that every citizen and every intellectual possesses. This implies honoring the principles of being a good person, a good citizen, and the values that go with these. Nonetheless, it is the choice of the individual in current or future generations, whether he/she chooses to disregard these responsibilities or chooses to live as the citizen of another country.

It is the choice of the individual in current or future generations whether he/she has a Turkish citizen as spouse. In case this spouse works in our institutions in an area where he/she has expertise, then the conditions for spouse employment apply equally, without regard to color, religion, or race.

The responsibilities of current and future generation family members are defined in the following way and they are of paramount importance. In any generation, it should not be the cause of dishonor for our institutions if a member of the family, or his/her kin, does not conform to these responsibilities. Utmost care must be taken to introduce successive generations to these responsibilities.

Standards and Expectations Concerning Family Members

Upbringing of Children

Family members must explain to their offspring; the values and responsibilities of the family, the duties and rules of authority and status as executives of family institutions, and issues related to the use and distributions of resources, and make an effort to transparently, pedagogically, and psychologically prepare their offspring to adopt these principles. The expectations of the family members during all processes must be confined to the principles and standards contained within the boundaries defined above. In case the Family Council is concerned that the values of the core family of an individual do not conform to the values expressed in this Constitution, then individual's legal rights associated with being a shareholder are retained, but privilege of management is terminated.

As the family expands, differences will arise naturally. Difference in goals, abilities and competencies, worldviews, values, and perspective on business life and life philosophies should be expected. It would be wrong to act as if there are no differences, as if everyone thinks like founder–entrepreneur and as if everyone is a natural manager of the family business. It would also not be appropriate to appoint individuals without regard to their individual personalities and different qualities, just as it would not be appropriate to treat them as "heirs" to the family business. What is appropriate instead is that care should be taken to achieve a fit between the needs of the business and abilities of family members, and to cultivate the individual if there is a fit on both sides.

Support for Personal Development and Wealth Education

Success of the family business develops in accordance with the shared vision of family members. The personal development of new generations should be supported under the leadership of the Family Council, with the planning of education and development in knowledge of property rights, the vision of the family business, and related topics. Young members of the family should be made to feel that the family business is not a privilege but a responsibility. A group approved by the Family Council should plan a wealth education process for each member of the family. During this education, effort should be made to instill a sense of self-respect, citizenship knowledge, and a positive approach. Wealth education should convey knowledge about the family, the business, and family values to the next generation. Wealth education does not prepare young family members for management careers in the family business; it teaches then the values that will be the basis of their future.

Distribution of Family Resources

General Principles

1. The distribution of profits arising from the operations of the institutions mentioned in this Constitution and any future institution that might be established and added to the family organizations shall be in the following manner: Every generation receives the share that the previous generation legally entitles them to receive (e.g., Second Generation receives what the First Generation legally entitles them, Third Generation receives what the Second Generation legally entitles them, and so on).
2. Every shareholder is free to distribute his/her own share of profits to children. However, in case of establishing an equity relationship with an individual or legal entity from outside the family (such as partial of complete transfer of shares, participating in a capital increase etc.), absolute majority (100%) of the General Meeting of Shareholders and Board of Directors is required.
3. Shareholders may work in the family institutions. In that case, they will receive a salary commensurate with those of other professionals who do that job. A shareholder who does not work in one of the family institutions cannot receive a salary.
4. It is undesirable for the spouse of a shareholder to work in one of the family institutions or an organization that has financial ties with family institutions. Effort must be made to avoid this situation. In certain situations, a service or product offered by a spouse may be transacted in line with fair market conditions.
5. The share of annual profits to be distributed as dividends is determined by legally authorized parties. The investments in R&D to improve the physical and academic condition of institutions should be prioritized when making this decision. Profits must be legally distributed after this figure is determined and educated.

Property, Inheritance, Sale, Marriage, and Divorce

Every member of the family should act in accordance with the principles contained in the Constitution and mind the following property issues in cases of inheritance, sale, marriage, and divorce.

The shares of the family should not be sold to outside parties, defiantly not to competing businesses. Prior to transactions mentioned in the title, every care should be taken to ensure that the shares are not transferred to third parties.

In cases of divorce, the spouse with no blood relation to the family loses the title and rights associated with being a member of the family.

Working Principles for Family Members

The status of family members (working in the business and in management) regarding power and position:

The main principle concerning how to determine which family member will be endowed with which power is "the possession of that individual of the qualities, abilities and experience for the position for which he/she is considered." This principle should be upheld in place of other considerations, such as being older, being a shareholder, or having more shares.

Argun Gazi and Ece Gazi (as the Second Generation) have initially used age as the criterion for distribution of power among the Third Generation. Three years was determined as the length of time to hold power and started to rotate members of that generation. For successive generations, distribution of power will be maintained with under the light of principles set forth above and with the decision of the Family Council.

If there is more than one shareholder possessing similar qualities, Family Council decides.

Care should be taken to ensure that conflict does not arise between shareholders in cases of deliberate transfer of power as a result of unexpected and unwelcome events (such as health). In such situations, shareholders should produce solutions in accordance with the values set forth in the Values section of this Constitution.

Distribution of Jobs and Positions

The issue of which management position will be matched with which shareholder will be resolved with reference to the career desires and skills of the individual and needs of the business. For obtaining a position, it should not be sufficient to be a shareholder and successive generations should be made to know this. Prior generations should act in ways that would set an example for successive generations.

Distribution of Authority and Responsibility

Generally, assembly of shareholders (general assembly meetings) are in charge economically and managerially. However, Family Council is the only authority at a higher level.

The general assembly meetings of shareholders of all companies (businesses) ensure that business is conducted in line with management principles and in contemporary legal ways. In practice, financial and managerial responsibility rests with Boards of Directors at companies and schools, and with the Board of Trustees at Eskisehir University.

Assemblies of shareholders of companies distribute authority and responsibility to suitable cadres for monitoring revenues, costs, budgets, profits and losses, cash flows, financial, and legal practice, at times by employing professional expert consultants. In addition, managerial practices at companies reflect the distribution of authority and responsibility through the same objective procedure.

Family Council and Its Working Principles

Family Council is a gathering for the discussion and resolution of issues related to the business and the family. The primary function of the Family Council is to identify and preserve the prioritized values, needs, expectations from the business and institutions, and develop policies to protect the long-term interests of the family.

Every member of the family is a natural member of the Family Council. Being a shareholder is not a requirement to participate. Shareholders at family businesses and institutions, who are not members of the family, cannot participate. Minimum age to attend the Family Council is 18; whereas the minimum age to vote is 25.

Meetings with the Family Council, which convene with working and nonworking members of the family, should be informative. Family Council sessions should be held with a prior agenda, in a sincere atmosphere, with a predictable interval of twice a year, except extraordinary sessions, and minutes of the meeting should be kept. Initially, the leader and President of the Family Council is Argun Gazi, the founding leader of the family business. In subsequent periods, the President of the Family Council will be a member of the eldest generation and employed by one of the companies or institutions. The atmosphere of the Family Council should always reflect the fact that responsibility for the unity and integrity of the family rests with individual family members.

Duties of the Family Council

1. Educates, warns. makes suggestions, takes decisions, and proposes penalties in matters related to the rights and responsibilities about management of property. While making decisions, ordinary decisions require a simple majority, while extraordinary decisions require a three-quarters majority.
2. Helps to determine the boundaries between family and business.
3. Presents the opportunity for family members, individuals employed or not employed by the business to express opinions and be informed about the business.
4. Provides a platform to discuss problems of the family (education, health, retirement, sale etc.).
5. Decides how power will be transferred inline with the principles contained in Article VIII.C.1.
6. Is the supreme organ in making this Constitution operational and monitors the decisions and penalties while they are implemented.

Various Additional Clauses

It is expected that family members will treat all Family Council issues in strict confidentiality.

To amend any of the articles contained in this Constitution, a 100% majority is required.

The Constitution shall become effective with the signature of the Founders.

Learning Notes

The reader of this constitution/case should come away with the sense that this family has attempted to deal with a variety of contingencies that could be faced by the family and the firm going forward. This includes divorce, generations who did not wish to be involved with the firm in the future. It should also be obvious to the reader that the family placed a higher value on providing quality education through their profit and nonprofit educational operations than they did on making money. It is interesting that they have also enshrined the principles of Ataturk, the founder of the modern Turkish nation as a part of their value statement. What may not have been clear is that the leaders of the firm, the Founders of the Constitution, are all women.

Chapter 5
Case Three: Surviving Revolution, But Succumbing to Succession – The Story of Five Siblings

This case was researched and developed by Janelle Fernandez and was written under the supervision of Alan Carsrud and Malin Brännback. This case examines how families can survive terrible economic and political turmoil and ultimately succumb to the ravages of family turf wars and intrigue. While not typical of the external crises that hit most firms, it is typical of the kinds of issues that occur when the succession process is lacking planning or totally ignored.

The Roots

All firms have a beginning with high hopes and bright futures and this was certainly the case for Groupo Cubano Corporation which was founded in 1949 in Havana, Cuba by the young engineer and entrepreneur, Mario Garcia de Lara. That same year, at age 25, he married Maria Miret y Gomez, the daughter of a wealthy Mexican plantation owner and politically connected Cuban mother. With his wife's encouragement, Mario brought his ideas into fruition and set off on a journey of the Garcia family with Maria which he would not forget.

With his father-in-law's financial help and is mother-in-law's politically connected family, Groupo Cubano began as a construction company that grew rapidly as any entrepreneur dreams their venture will do. Among its initial large projects, was the airport in the city of Santiago de Cuba. Shortly after that it won the contract for one of the major highways spanning the island from Santiago de Cuba to Havana and beyond. In the process, Groupo Cubano acquired many other industries, including a pencil factory, a toilet and bathroom accessory factory, and several textile plants. By the late 1957, he owned one of only two steel mills in Cuba at the time. Nelson Rockefeller, later Vice President of the United States, was one of Mario's two business partners in the steel venture that came into fruition shortly before Mario's unwanted, untimely and yet necessary departure from Cuba.

A.L. Carsrud and M. Brännback, *Family Firms in Transition: Case Studies on Succession,* 25
Inheritance, and Governance, SpringerBriefs in Business 3,
DOI 10.1007/978-1-4614-1201-4_5, © Alan L. Carsrud and Malin Brännback, 2011

Within its first 5 years, Groupo Cubano became among the top revenue-earning conglomerates in Cuba, with net income at over 100 million Cuban pesos in 1955. The once-struggling Mario Garcia was rubbing shoulders and elbows with the richest of the rich in Cuba and those who came down to Cuba for the winters from the United States. He and his beautiful wife were regulars at the night clubs in Havana and even maintained a suite at the swank National Hotel. Mario Garcia was the third richest man in all of Cuba at the time. For all of the trappings of wealth, Mario still put in long hours at work overseeing his rapidly growing group of firms.

But life was about to change with the Cuban Revolution. Fidel Castro's militia began to seek out "donations" from those who were "in favor of the revolution." This was not the case for Mario, who was a strong and vocal adversary of Castro, his followers, and any sort of revolution that would threaten his business and way of life. He was not alone, his in-laws likewise did not support the revolution and besides his mother-in-law was a part of the ruling families of Cuba. He opposed contributing any money to Castro's cause despite the suggestions that it would be dangerous to not support Castro. Once Castro's power increased and the Communist government began to seize businesses, Mario, a man known for his stubbornness, did not flee nor back down in his opposition to the Revolution. He fought the new government with words and money till word came from a former partner came that Mario and his family would be killed if he did not flee the country. He was forced to abandon all that he had built in order to save himself and his family from persecution, or worse.

Leaving Cuba

Within a day of making the decision to leave, Mario left for Mexico via Panama through an arrangement with a high level official in the Panamanian embassy in Havana. This was May 4, 1959. He traveled alone so as to not risk the safety of his wife and children. In early June, 1959, Maria, pregnant with their fifth child, left Cuba with her four children aged 11 months to 8 years, for Mexico. Because her father was a Mexican citizen, she and her children had Mexican passports and were able to leave the country. However, they were stripped of all their Cuban assets, including property, jewelry, artwork, and cash. Maria arrived in Mexico with no money, pregnant, and with four young children. She stayed with her father in his country home in Oaxaca until Mario was able to join them. Soon after Mario rejoined his family, he moved them, with help of friends, to Puerto Rico to "wait out" what they thought would be a temporary Castro regime.

A Little Bit of Foresight Goes a Long Way

Maria's father, Juan Domingo Miret de Cordoba knew what Castro and his men were capable of in terms of dealing with "enemies of the state." He had been through the Spanish Civil War as a Republican and knew first hand what it was like to lose everything. He had advised his daughter just prior to the start of the revolution to secure some of their assets in an off-shore account. Mario, stubborn as ever, opposed the idea and brushed his wife's suggestions off as foolish. Fortunately, Maria ignored her husband and transferred $200,000 to an account in the Bank of New York.

To Mario's surprise, when he learned of the money, he flew to New York City with nothing but an account number and a security code written on a piece of paper to retrieve the money. Those $200,000 were what the Garcia family of seven would live off of and rebuild from during the next 4 years. Maria always knew her father would be there to help the family out. Only later, when Maria's father died in Mexico, did she learn that her beloved father left the bulk of his estate to his son, Juan Pedro. In a note to her in his will he said he felt that he had more than provided for his oldest daughter by helping her husband get started in Cuba.

Frustration in Puerto Rico

Thinking that Puerto Rico was going to be much like pre-revolutionary Cuba, Mario decided he would try his entrepreneurial luck on this Spanish speaking island not far from Cuba. However, Mario forgot that one of the secrets to his success in Cuba had been the backing of his wealthy father-in-law and his Cuban mother-in-law's extensive family connections. Regardless, he immediately started a firm in an industry for which he had little direct experience. Yet, his Midas touch seemed to have failed him. This failed business endeavor was the result of his notorious habit in investing in random businesses that caught his eye. He had partnered with a couple other Cuban refugees and setup a slipper factory in San Juan. From the start his partners kept draining the firm's accounts and they did not know how to market their footwear to stores in the United States. The reality set in that the Garcia's were running out of the money Maria had put into the Bank of New York a few years earlier. Mario ended up selling his portion to one of the other partners in the venture at a huge loss. Discouraged they looked to find new options.

Starting Over in Miami

Mario, Maria, and their children were unhappy in Puerto Rico not only because of their failed business venture but also because they had no family nearby. Mario's recent business failure colored his view of San Juan and his opportunities there, while Maria yearned for an extended family like she had in Cuba. Finding neither an adequate job nor a profitable business, they decided as a family to move to Miami exactly 2 years from the time they had arrived in San Juan. Fortunately, they were able to join other members of their extended families in Miami; Mario's mother and sister had been able to flee Cuba as well. While not wealthy, they had managed to get some money out of Cuba prior to Castro's takeover. They had bought a little house in the Little Havana area of Miami and offered for Mario, Maria, and the children to stay with them till they could get settled in South Florida.

Using the last of the funds Maria had secured in New York, Mario started upon yet another new business venture. Because of his previous success, he decided to establish another construction company. At least he knew this industry and used his engineering skills gained from being a student at the University of Havana. Since the Garcias had five offspring, they decided to incorporate the company as Siblings Construction Corporation. This venture was successful and continues to be the Garcia family's main source of income to this day. Because the firm had an Anglo sounding name, many people in the city viewed it as an "American" firm, while those in the Cuban community in Miami knew of Mario's reputation in pre-revolutionary Havana.

Mario's primary investment for Siblings was in real estate. Initially, he bought two large plots of land in the city of Sweetwater, a suburb west of downtown Miami, and built 40 duplexes on the properties. Siblings owned and operated the duplexes they rented primarily to other Cuban immigrants. The entire Garcia family was involved in everything from bookkeeping to renting the units. One task Mario took as his own was collecting the rent. Mario demanded that tenants pay in cash and physically collected rent on the 1st or 15th of the month. The company's monthly gross income was $60,000. Mario thought that finally the bad times were over. Besides, he had a son so he could leave this new business to if and when he decided to retire.

Family Troubles

Mario's only son, Mario Jr., turned out to be, what many in the local Cuban exile community called "…a bad apple." Much to his father's chagrin and being rebellious against his parents' wishes, he made it obvious he did not want to work for the family business. He chose instead to get into some bad business ventures with some others looking for a quick dollar and big trouble. South Florida, long known for local corruption and shady deals, still had a dislike for embezzlement of their fellow Cuban immigrants. In the early 1980s, Mario, Jr. got into, what his mother called "…a bit of trouble with the law."

The family was forced to sell some of their rental properties to complete the bail money necessary to get the younger Mario out of jail. In the end, the family helped him repay over $2 million to keep him from a long jail term. Maria claims the family business still was never able to recover the profits from the loss of those properties. Disappointed at their son's actions and his lack of communication with them, further strained the relationship between the elder Garcia and their son. They lost touch and as a result, they did not even meet their grandson Matthew, until he was already 4 years old.

Finding a Successor

Mario finally was wise enough to know that his oldest son was not appropriate to take over the family business. As the proud grandfather of eight intelligent grandchildren, he knew that they would not disappoint him as his son already had.

Mario chose his second and fourth eldest grandchildren and groomed them to take over the business. The boy, Rick, would take over the property management and day-to-day operations, while the girl, Vicky, who was studying law at the University of Florida in Gainesville, would take over the administrative functions. The company's annual reports at the time (2001) had six members of the family as officers. These included Lucy, Rick's mom, Brenda, and Vicky's mom. Rick, and Vicky were listed as Vice Presidents of Siblings Construction Corp. The elder Garcias, Mario and Maria, were listed as President, and Secretary. While not back to the wealth they enjoyed in Cuba, the Garcias were comfortable with a home in Coral Gables and a small apartment for weekends at Miami Beach.

Grandchildren in the Business

Because Mario still believed in personally picking up the rent in cash from the apartments that he own, he had structured the business as primarily a cash business. However, Mario was getting older and his health was starting to deteriorate. Finally Mario and Maria asked two of their grandsons, Rick and Michael, if they would go and pick up the rent for their grandfather every month. They would also show available units to potential tenants and hire repairmen to fix any problems or complaints. It was looking like Mario might finally let go of the business and turn it over to the next generation for leadership.

At this time, Rick was 21 and Michael, had just turned 18 years old. By this point, Mario was doing nothing more than overseeing the bookkeeping and finances of the business, but continued to have the ultimate say in important decisions. Rick, to whom he was closest, often was referred to by his grandmother as the one slated to be the manager of the business as soon as his Mario Sr. was ready to officially pass the torch.

However, having his own ideas, Rick was studying Real Estate Management at the University of Miami, with hopes of opening his own property management company. He did not always agree with the decisions of his grandfather concerning the rental business and knew he could become a successful real estate entrepreneur like an increasing number of Cuban Americans in South Florida.

More Turmoil Occurs

In early 2005, Rick began dating an older woman whom he met at a bar on Lincoln Road on South Beach. Her name was Vivian Schwartz. She was 30, divorced, and Jewish. If her family had been a Jewish family from Cuba, Rick's family might have felt differently. Mario, a devote Catholic, was adamantly against his grandson dating this "person." He questioned her sincerity and the constant disagreements between he and Rick about her presence strained their relationship severely. Moreover, Mario was beginning to suspect that Rick was taking money from the company. He was treating his girlfriend to lavish trips and expensive gifts when he had no other source of income except his mediocre weekly paycheck. Rick denied the allegations and managed to calm his grandfather's suspicions and persuade him otherwise. His grandmother, Maria, was distraught at the thought of another member of the family being "disowned" by her husband Mario.

By late 2005, Rick had the "last straw" about his grandfather's distaste for Vivian. He finally confronted Mario and claimed that he would marry her without any sort of prenuptial agreement. Mario, furious and impulsive, decided to terminate any rights Rick had to the business. He did this by telling the rest of the family that he had disowned Rick. Rick and his mother Lucy (one of Mario's daughters) were angry at the ordeal and did not speak to Mario for nearly 12 months. They did not seek to reconcile until Mario was hospitalized with severe emphysema. Maria felt increasingly isolated from her children and grandchildren. In the mean time, Michael, the younger grandson, had been collecting the rent with his father John, Mario and Maria's son-in-law. Mario and Maria oversaw the finances with the help of their daughter Brenda. Vicky, the grand-daughter was now an attorney practicing in Miami. She had begun managing all legal issues Siblings Construction needed handled, such as tenant evictions.

Poor Planning and Death

Mario Garcia's business sense and personal character were very old fashioned. He believed that deals could still be made and upheld with a simple handshake. He believed real estate professionals never went back on their word. His family sometimes felt he was very arrogant and did not like to seek advice on his dealings. He was constantly reminding them of their wealth in Cuba and that someday he would recover that wealth. He also believed he would live to see Fidel Castro dead and he would outlive the Castro brothers. As a result, he did not plan his succession within the business. In fact, he had no written document to secure his wishes for the future of the company he built. He said the children and his wife knew what he wanted done. In April, 2006, at age 82, Mario Garcia passed away at South Miami Hospital of heart failure. He left no trusts, and no detailed will. Maria (81 years old) was left to manage their estate. Maria was in increasingly frail health. She had many decisions to make, including whether to sell the business, or choose one of her children or grandchildren to manage it and ultimately, inherit it. She looked to her closest daughter, Lucy, for advice.

More Problems Arise

Mario's death brought the Garcia family close together for a 2 week period. The children who had not spoken to their parents in years, Mario Jr., Lupe, and Martha came to his bedside during his last hours and surrounded their mother following his passing away. A couple of them had not spoken to each other in years. Maria at one point claimed that the only good thing that came from the death of her husband was that her family was back together again.

After the tears dried, however, the reunion was much more short-lived than Maria would have liked. Most of the children and grandchildren wanted a piece of the family firm and were sure that their grandfather's last testament would "divide the pie" as Mario, Jr. said. Because Rick had fought with his grandfather before his death and been "disowned," Michael thought he would continue running the business, as he had for the past months since his cousin's departure from Siblings Construction. Rick thought that since his grandfather no longer had any say, he would go back to managing the business, regardless of him being engaged to the woman his grandfather never approved of before his death. He was very close to his grandmother and knew that she would oblige his wish.

The other male cousin, Arthur, also saw his return home from the University of Florida and the timing of his grandfather's death as his personal opportunity to become a part of the family business. Encouraged by his mother Martha (who had been estranged from her parents for the past 5 years), he asked his grandmother if she wanted him to stay with her after Mario's death. Maria reluctantly agreed. Arthur stayed with his aging grandmother for a few months. He then received a job offer in investment banking and quickly moved to New York City to work for Lehman Brothers. In the meantime, Rick also started living with his grandmother, not trusting Arthur's intentions.

Who Will Own and Run the Business?

Maria was left with many decisions, one of which was who was going to run the business. She also had to deal with the perplexing issue of who would own the firm after her death given that Mario's will left the entire firm to her. After much coercion from her youngest (and admittedly favorite) daughter, Lucy, Maria asked Rick to return to running the business. Rick immediately fired Michael, bringing animosity from Michael's sister Vicky, who Mario had always said would inherit the family business with Rick.

To visually solidify his position, Rick moved in to Maria's house in Coral Gables, and took over his grandfather's office. Brenda, Michael, and Vicky's mother, enraged at the unfair ousting of her son from the company, stopped talking to her sister Lucy, her nephew Rick, and her mother, Maria. Vicky, enraged as well, stood up for her brother Michael but was unwilling to end the relationship with her grandmother. She had once been very close to her cousin Rick, but that relationship continued to fade by the minute. She was disillusioned with his obsession to have full control of the business and his staking claim on what she believed was never 100% rightfully his.

Everyone seemed to ignore the reality that the business was now Maria's, including Vicky. Ironically enough, Vicky did not attempt to pursue legal action. She believed that pursuing any type of legal action would ruin her relationship with her grandmother and she did not want to risk it. She also feels proud of her success as an attorney and wants to make her own *statement* demonstrating that she does not *need* the business to live.

Reorganization of the Business

In 2007, Siblings Construction Corporation filed their annual report with the state of Florida. In this report, they had removed both Brenda and Vicky from the list of corporate officers. There was no board meeting or vote to remove them. Rick filed the annual report without their names. The report had Maria Garcia as president, Rick Perez as Secretary/Treasurer, and Lucy Garcia as Vice President. In the 2008 annual report, Rick added Mario Perez, his younger brother, as another Vice President of the business.

Currently, the business continues to be managed by Rick Perez. He has hired one person to oversee the maintenance of their rental properties and allows that person to live in one of the units for free. Additionally, he has finally graduated from the University of Miami with his real estate degree and started his own property management company. However, business is not going smooth for Rick with Siblings Corporation. Rick has been dependent on his income from Siblings to pay his bills and he continues to live with this grandmother. He has not been able to pay property taxes on the firm's rental properties on time for the past 2 years because of the recession and renters behind on their payments. Siblings Corporation currently owes Miami-Dade County over $50,000 in back-taxes.

Future of the Business

There have been discussions between Rick and his grandmother about selling the business. Due to the falling housing economy in Miami and around the country, however, it is not an optimal time to sell the properties. Selling all the duplexes could potentially pay off all of the company's debt and support the grandmother for the rest of her life. Additionally, it would leave Rick with a large quantity of money in his pocket if he can get his grandmother to agree that half the business is his. Maria has a lot to consider and with her declining health, not much time in which to do it.

Learning Notes

1. Did you think Mario planned his succession well? Is not, why?
2. Did Rick treat his other family members fairly in this matter? Could Mario have built a succession plan that would have kept the family from being in such turmoil?
3. Could Maria have done anything differently to change the family situation? If so, what?

Chapter 6
Case Four: Dodger Baseball – The End of Family-Owned Major League Baseball

Ilene Resnick and Thomas Murray provided the initial research for this case which was edited by Pablo Brezman and Colleen Robb. The final writing was under the supervision of Alan Carsrud and Malin Brännback. The names and information in this case are real and the case is based upon information from public sources and no information was provided by the firm and the individuals involved.

Introduction: January, 1997

"The time is approaching when a family cannot support a major league baseball team. It's a time of corporate ownership. All economic factors figure into this. Family ownership is a dying breed. It's a high-risk business, as high as the oil business. You need a broader base than an individual family to carry you through the storms."[1] With this statement, Peter O'Malley announced that the Dodger's baseball team was up for sale in 1997. The Dodgers franchise composed of several baseball teams, a training facility in Florida, and Dodger Stadium in Los Angeles. The Dodgers ballclub had won six World Series Championship titles. In the 26 years that Peter O'Malley had been president of the ball club, they had reached the World Series 18 times. The highest price for a major league team to date was $173 million, yet experts were quoted in the press[2] as expecting the price for this team at between $300 and 500 million due to the caliber of the organization. The Dodgers had drawn in a total of over 2 million fans/year for the last 24 consecutive years[3] and 3 million fans annually 11 times.

---

[1] "Baseballs blue sale; After almost 50 years of owning the Dodgers, the O'Malleys take themselves out of the ball game" *Time Magazine*, published January 20, 1997.
[2] "Baseballs blue sale; After almost 50 years of owning the Dodgers, the O'Malleys take themselves out of the ball game" *Time Magazine*, published January 20, 1997.
[3] "Peter O'Malley puts Dodgers up for sale" *Sportsline USA*, Internet NewsWire January 6, 1997.

A.L. Carsrud and M. Brännback, *Family Firms in Transition: Case Studies on Succession,*   33
Inheritance, and Governance, SpringerBriefs in Business 3,
DOI 10.1007/978-1-4614-1201-4_6, © Alan L. Carsrud and Malin Brännback, 2011

The Ownership Legacy[4]

In 1912, Ebbets Field, a baseball stadium which seated 25,000 at the time, was constructed for the Brooklyn Dodgers in Brooklyn, New York. Part of the construction deal involved Dodgers' president, Charles Ebbets, selling of 50% of the Dodgers franchise for a hefty $100,000 to brothers Edward and Steve McKeever, whose contracting company was in charge of the stadium's construction. During the Brooklyn Dodgers' 1925 season, Ebbets fell ill and died the morning of April 18 in New York. Ebbets was 66 years old. Eleven days later, Edward McKeever passed away due to a cold, which he reportedly caught at Ebbets's funeral. The ballclub became controlled by Stephen McKeever and the executors of the Ebbets Estate, and they elected Wilbert Robinson as the new president. Stephen McKeever himself becomes president of the Dodgers less than 5 years later in 1930.

Within 2 years, McKeever died, leaving his stake in the ballclub to his daughter, Mrs. Dearie Mulvey and her husband, James, who was president of Samuel Goldwyn Productions. In 1938, former Cincinatti Reds GM Leland "Larry" MacPhail became president, and after winning a National League Championship in 1941, MacPhail went to serve in the U.S. Army. In 1942, former St. Louis Cardinals General Manager Branch Rickey stepped up to the position of the Dodgers' president.

Partnering with Walter O'Malley and Andrew Schmitz, Branch decided to purchase 25% of the Dodgers from the Ebbets Estate for a price of $347,000. After obtaining another 50% of the Dodgers in 1945, each of the three partners controlled an equal 25% of the Dodgers. In 1950, O'Malley bought Branch's 25% of the franchise, now controlling half of the ballclub shares and O'Malley then became president of the Dodgers.

Five years later, John Lawrence Smith died, leaving his shares to his wife and in 1948, O'Malley purchased those shares from her to give him 66% ownership. At the same time, James and Dearie Mulvey decided to increase their ownership of the franchise to 33%. That same year, the Brooklyn Dodgers became the Los Angeles Dodgers when the team made a highly publicized move to the west coast. O'Malley's primary reason for moving to the west coast was his desire to build a more modern stadium for his ball players and New York City officials had not been able to satisfy O'Malley with an appropriate site for the stadium O'Malley had in mind.

As O'Malley continued his pursuit of total ownership of the Dodgers, O'Malley's son, Peter, had meanwhile been working his way up through the Dodgers management franchise. From childhood, he had dreamed of working for the Dodgers and one day becoming owner and president, like his father. In 1962, Peter was named the director of Dodgertown, the Dodgers' spring training headquarters located in Vero Beach, FL. In 1965, Peter became president of the Spokane Indians baseball team, which in 1958 had been awarded the Los Angeles Triple-A franchise to begin

---

[4] "Important dates in Dodger history by the Associated Press" *Sportsline USA*, Internet NewsWire January 6, 1997. This article provided ownership trade details and dates.

play in the minor league, Pacific Coast League (PCL). Peter led the Indians to their 1970 PCL Championship title with 26 games and an impressive clean sweep of the league's championship series.

The same year of the PCL title, Walter O'Malley became chairman of the board for the Dodgers and his son Peter graciously accepted his succession as president of the Dodgers. Five years later, Walter O'Malley had finally acquired the remaining 33% of the Dodgers to own 100% of the franchise. As a full owner and chairman, Walter would remain actively involved with the Dodgers for the rest of his life. Unfortunately, that end came fairly soon. Less than a month after his wife's death in July, 1979, Walter O'Malley also passed away, leaving ownership of the Dodgers to his two children, Peter O'Malley and Terry Seidler.

Peter O'Malley has lived up to his father's legacy well, as an active promoter of baseball around the globe serving as a director of the Los Angeles World Affairs Council.[5] His civic involvement included serving on the Board of Governors of the Los Angeles County Music Center, being a director of the Amateur Athletic Foundation and serving as president of the Little League Baseball Foundation. However, Peter, unlike his father's gregarious nature, has a careful quiet manner, and on the whole, avoids the public eye. Peter does have a talent for brilliant and extensive team promotions. It is these promotional strategies that have helped link the franchise into many sectors of the community and it has been attributed as one of the key reasons the fans love "Dodger Blue."

The O'Malley's 47 years of family ownership of a baseball team is surpassed only by the Yawkey Family,[6] who purchased the Boston Red Sox in 1933 (Yawkey sold 25% of the team in 1977). As recently as 1980, various families owned ten baseball teams,[7] now less than five are family businesses. Twenty-two teams out of twenty-eight have been sold since 1982, some more than once. The O'Malleys are the only team owners that have no other business (see Addenda 1 for the ownership profiles as of 1985).[8]

Dodger Way

The *Dodger Way*[9] is famous in baseball circles. The Dodgers' management team treats their players lavishly and they expect top performance from them in return. The management team is a cohesive unit, with many former Dodgers legends, including

---

[5]"Important dates in Dodger history by the Associated Press" *Sportsline USA*, Internet NewsWire January 6, 1997. This article provided ownership trade details and dates.

[6]"Peter O'Malley puts Dodgers up for sale" *Sportsline USA*, Internet NewsWire January 6, 1997.

[7]"Potential bidders stepping up to the plate" *The Los Angeles Times*, published January 8, 1997.

[8]"The L.A. Dodgers history; Its' hits, runs and errors" *The Christian Science Monitor*, published January 13, 1997.

[9]"The Dodger way; here's scoop in how O'Malley made his team a little special" *The Los Angeles Times*, published January 9, 1997.

Manny Mota, Reggie Smith, and Rick Monday, now working for the ballclub off the field. Many famous Dodger veterans often come out to special events and practices to share their insights, such veterans as Don Drysdale and Steve Garvey are often seen at Dodger practices. Along with the expertise of the great Walter Alston and Tommy Lasorda, each serving as head coach for over 20 years, the members of the organization form lifetime relations to the Dodgers. The relations within the Dodgers extend the O'Malley family to include many individuals, all of whom are sharing in the quest for baseball excellence.

The difference in the *Dodger Way* is most obviously observed while the team is traveling on the road. The Dodgers were the only team with their own jet, which was sold only after the pilot died. The Dodger franchise covered the expenses for all the immediate family members to travel with every player on the team to any away game they wanted to attend while most other Major League Baseball (MLB) teams only sent players and staff. The Dodgers reserved 100 rooms in their hotels, while other teams make do with about 25. To keep the team's players in shape over the winter holidays, a 3 day a week winter workout schedule is provided to each player which includes aerobics training plus full pitching, fielding, and batting practice sessions. The culture and social events for the Dodgers are also extensive, an example of which was a team vacation to Europe in 1988. In addition to the many perks, large and expensive parties are held every year throughout the year, including a Christmas party during spring training, a western barbecue in the summer, and a St. Patrick's Day bash.

Players are not the only employees of the Dodger franchise that benefit from the *Dodger Way*. While other MLB teams change their managers annually, the Dodgers have had only three different general managers since 1954. Many players stay on the Dodger team as advisors long after retiring from the field. The organization is full of famous players, including Sandy Colfax and Ron Cey, all of whom have aided the Dodgers win championships and the players' heart stay in touch with the game. Another example of the Dodgers' unfaltering consistency and quality is Vin Scully, the famous voice of the Dodgers, who has been doing the Dodgers' play-by-play announcing since 1950.

In addition to treating the players and employees well, Peter O'Malley has refused to commercialize the team. No advertisements are allowed in the outfield and only a few limited merchandise product lines are deemed with the Dodgers' logos. And, most importantly, Peter has kept ticket prices to the Dodgers games at a fraction of the prices to other sporting events in Los Angeles. In fact, the Dodgers have the lowest ticket prices of any MLB team.[10] A season ticket behind home plate at a Dodgers game has a face value of $12, while an equivalent ticket for the Los Angeles Lakers National Basketball League team has a face value of $47.

The Dodgers' stadium is also not exploited the way other MLB stadiums are. The Dodgers' stadium is used for about 80 home games/year plus less than 20 dates for other income producing events, with no adjacent theaters, restaurants, or other year-round on-site income producing enterprises. The Dodgers make it a policy to

---

[10] "Dodger's consistency set standard" *The Outlook*, published January 7, 1997.

avoid generating more profits if there is a risk of identity misuse, which is what many other teams see as conventional ways to earn a profit.

The Farm System

A widely used recruiting system used in professional baseball is what is called a "farm system," by which major league clubs, through ownership and affiliation, are able to control their minor league teams, which are typically stocked with large numbers of players subject to long-term reserve clause requirements. The farm system is actually accredited as being perfected by former Dodger-owner, Branch Rickey. Hence, the Dodgers have been admired for having the best farm system in MLB.

The Dodgers' ability to use the farm system to their advantage strengthened the Dodgers control over its baseball players in a number of ways. First, being bound by the reserve clause, players in the minor league system had no choice but to stay within that team's system or leave professional baseball altogether. Second, low minor league salaries helped pressure major league players to reduce their own salary demands, lest they lose their jobs to a minor league player willing to work at the major league level for less. Third, major league owners were able to sell the contracts of minor league players bound by reserve clauses.[11]

The Dodges have been able to take full advantage of their farm system. In fact, the Dodgers seldom used free agents and have developed nearly all their champion players from within the organization.[12] The Dodgers' reliance on the farm system coupled with the Dodgers' fraternity-like culture has assured smooth transitions from the minors to the majors for most of the Dodgers' players. The Dodgers have enjoyed financial benefits of this system as well, avoiding high salaries for top performers by their long-term contracts, while the culture helps to instill a sense of duty in everyone to keep the system developing success year after year.

The Dodger organization owns[13] the Vero Beach Dodgers (Florida State A League), the Santo Domingo Dodgers (Dominican Republic Summer League), and the La Romana Dodgers (another Dominican Republic Summer League team). In addition, the team has scouts worldwide and has opened a new baseball academy in San Joaquin, Venezuela. The team has working agreements, a type of strategic alliance, with the Albuquerque Dukes (Pacific Coast AAA League), the San Antonio Missions (Texas AA League), the San Bernadino Stampede (California A League), the Savannah Sand Gnats (South Atlantic A League), Yakima Bears (Northwest A League), and the Great Falls Dodgers (Pioneer League). All of these teams all contribute to the Dodger farm system, lowering salaries and providing new major leaguers season after season.

---

[11] "Baseball Fans and Communities Protection Act of 1994" *House Report No, 103-871.*

[12] "Q & A: Peter O'Malley" *The Los Angeles Times,* published March 24, 1987.

[13] 1996 Dodgers Media Guide, The Los Angeles Dodgers, published 1996.

League Control

The MLB association is composed of 30 teams divided into 2 leagues, 14 in the American League and 16 in the National League. The owner's association manages the MLB. Unique to this business is an exemption from anti-trust regulations (the only industry in America to be exempt). The players have a union which administrates relations between the teams and players.

Walter O'Malley was well known as a key figure in the MLB association; some claim he selected two of the league's commissioners, General Eckert and Bowie Kuhn. Walter's son Peter has also become an essential voice in league decisions, though not usually as dominating as his father was in discussions, as his father often forced others to exceed expectations. Peter has, of course, faced a very different group of owners, many of whom have enormous financial resources. Peter's failed bid to go on the MLB executive committee, where his father had served for years,[14] demonstrated at least some owners don't think Peter's leadership is consistent with the industry's changing needs. The MLB has vowed to act as a cooperative enterprise, rather than a company that in the past had acquiesced to a demanding few.

The Owner's Family

Walter O'Malley was undoubtedly the most powerful force in baseball during his time with the Dodgers.[15] He was a self-made man from Flatbush, a small community in Brooklyn, New York. Peter, his son, grew up enjoying the luxuries his father's success provided to him. As Peter aged, the differences between him and his father grew to be quite distinct. While his father was outspoken, Peter was soft spoken. While Walter enjoyed the limelight, Peter was adverse to publicity. Peter was positioned from the beginning to take over the Dodgers one day. To prepare for this succession, Peter attended the Wharton School of Business and Finance in Pennsylvania to study business law.[16] During the summers, he worked at the minor leagues for the Dodgers in several staff positions, including camp counselor for the Dodgertown Camp for Boys in its initial year of 1954. Walter purposefully groomed his only son, Peter, for ultimately replacing him as the president for the Dodgers. Grooming his only son as his ultimate replacement for the presidency of the Dodgers, Walter kept Peter close to him and taught him everything he knew about the business of baseball. Peter himself fathered three children; Kevin, Brian, and Katherine. Kevin O'Malley, once believed by some as a future Dodger owner,[17] played baseball

---

[14] "So many reasons for him to sell" *The Outlook*, published January 7, 1997.

[15] "Inherit the wins" *The Los Angeles Times*, published January 7, 1997.

[16] *Who's who in professional baseball* by Gene Karst, Arlington House, published 1973.

[17] "Offspring training" *The Los Angeles Times*, published March 20, 1993.

at the University of Pennsylvania and also worked during summer break for the Dodgers along with his two siblings. But unlike his father, Kevin has no desire to ever run the team.

Terry Seidler was the only daughter of Walter O'Malley. Terry and her husband, Roland, also own 50% of the team while Peter owns the other half. When Walter moved the team to Los Angeles in 1948, Terry worked as her father's secretary throughout the transition. Since that time, she has remained, on the whole, uninvolved in the Dodger franchise. Terry and her husband have an astounding ten children, one of whom, Tom, is very interested in baseball. Tom Seidler has publicly indicated that he is very interested in and would remain involved in baseball, "whether it's with the Dodgers or some other team." Tom worked in the Dodger's marketing department after running the club's Class A affiliate in Great Falls, Montana in 1995.[18]

Dodger Stadium at Chavez Ravine

In 1948, when Walter O'Malley arrived in Los Angeles with his ballclub, he needed to build his stadium. In order to have Dodger's stadium built, Walter traded a 9 acre minor league park (Wrigley Field) for 315 acres north of downtown Los Angeles. The stadium seated 56,000 and came equipped with 16,000 parking spaces. The layout maximizes the audience's field of vision and is still admired today for its highly functional design. The stadium was ideal for baseball, and very few other vendors are given permission to use the facility. The present day drawbacks in the building are its age and its lack of access roads. Though an open air facility, the Dodgers have been rained out only 15 times since 1962. As the site is privately owned, the city will not pay for luxury boxes or other improvements often paid by bond issues in other cities.[19] In addition to baseball, the stadium has been used for concerts (Elton John, The Beatles, Michael Jackson, and the Three Tenors) and religious meetings (Billy Graham and Pope John Paul II). The 1984 Olympic Games used the stadium for exhibition baseball. Few other events need this size facility and some events that could be held here end up at Los Angeles Memorial Coliseum or Pasadena's Rose Bowl, each of which seat over 90,000.

Since 1995, Peter O'Malley has been planning a new National Football League (NFL) stadium to be built adjacent to Dodger Stadium. Though the NFL was in favor of its construction, the city council has insisted that the existing Los Angeles Coliseum Sports Arena, which was built in 1923 and seats just over 100,000 spectators, be the only football stadium in Los Angeles. The city council based the decision, in part, on the neighborhood's complaints of noise and traffic.

---

[18] "Dodger operation: Business as usual" *The Los Angeles Times*, published January 8, 1997.
[19] *1996 Dodgers Media Guide*, The Los Angeles Dodgers, published 1996.

Dodgertown and Campo Las Palmas

Vero Beach, Florida, has been home to the Dodgers for 49 consecutive years, longer than Los Angeles or Brooklyn. Dodgertown is the home of spring training for the Dodgers. The facility includes 450 acres, 2 golf courses (18 and 9 hole), a golf clubhouse, 45 golf course adjacent residences, 11 baseball training fields, the 6,500 seat Holman Stadium (dedicated in 1953), 90 units of housing, a 23,000 square foot administrative building (built in 1974), a 15,000 multipurpose building (built in 1990), and a conference center (180 person capacity). In addition, the facility has a pool and four tennis courts and a movie theater. Beside the sports facilities, 70 additional acres are used for citrus groves.

This massive facility was a former World War II Naval Air Station and is used annually by over 15 other professional sports teams from all over the globe. Five NFL teams have occasionally used the property to prepare for postseason games or preseason training. In addition, the Dodgers have a rookie camp in June and two adult fantasy baseball camps which showcase interaction with past and present Dodger heroes. The minor league Vero Beach Dodgers has used Dodgertown's Holman Stadium for the last 17 years. No other baseball team owns a spring training facility, let alone one as impressive as Dodgertown. Dodgertown has a peak staff of 450 people and a $3.5 million dollar payroll.[20] The year-round Dodgertown staff numbers over 250. The Dodger franchise also owns a baseball camp and small stadium in the Dominican Republic known as Campo Las Palmas. That facility is used by the Dodgers' two Dominican minor league teams.

Player Strife

In 1994, the player's union launched a strike for a total of 48 games. Several issues were at the heart of the confrontation, including salaries and player profit sharing. The team owners were insisting on salary caps, limiting the total team salaries, and the players were insisting on increased minimum salary amounts. At the end of the strike, little was resolved, but a 5-year agreement was signed. This agreement only delayed solving the problems, but did get the major league back in operation.

Player profit sharing occurs in other sports, but MLB team owners wanted to hold out for several reasons. The most obvious reason for the owners is a decrease in their profits. The second issue that surfaced in union negotiations was which sources of income would be included in this agreement: ticket sales, television rights, concessions sales, other merchandise licensing agreements, or trademark royalties. The most important issue to the majority of ballclub owners was the access by players and their agents to the ballclub's accounting records. This would give the

---

[20] "In Vero Beach, sale is hot topic" *The Los Angeles Times*, published January 15, 1997.

players and their agents the right to have records audited in case of disputes. This strike coupled with a declining industry raised tensions among the entire industry. Even if most teams within the league were profitable in a single year, the industry was showing a track record of losses. By 1992, as many as 50% of all MLB teams were losing money.[21]

The increasing number of baseball players acting as free agents has created a wage spiral with no end in sight. The Dodgers have been able to use the farm system to keep total team player salaries under $40 million (1995). However, many teams have relied on free agent players to help the team become instantly competitive. The savings in salaries via the farm system for the Dodgers are quite impressive when compared to the Florida Marlin's $117 million dollars spent on 1995 player salaries. The Baltimore Orioles led the American League in 1995 in salaries, but the $50 million payroll left them $5 million in the red.[22] At the time, the top paid player in the MLB was Albert Belle, who receives $11,000,000/year from the Chicago White Sox (5 year deal, 1997–2001). No team in MLB can afford both a well-financed farm system and top dollar salaries for free agent stars. Many MLB ballclubs are finding that it is the star players that fans will pay to see play, not minor league prospects.

Hollywood Buys Baseball

The O'Malley's make most of their money from the operations of the Dodgers. In contrast, Ted Turner, owner of the Atlanta Braves, makes money by using the team as programming for his cable network Turner Broadcasting System (TBS). Another company, the Tribune Company owns the Chicago Cubs and is able to use the team's activities as a source of entertainment in its television stations and exclusive news stories to sell the Chicago Tribune newspaper. Recently, the Disney Company bought a part of the California Angles, in part, to tie in with a series of movies beginning with "Angels in the Outfield." Disney also owns a hockey arena, the Anaheim Pond, which is right across the street from Angeles Stadium, where its team "The Mighty Ducks" ties in with a series of three movies with the same name. The trend toward corporate ownership is in every professional sport in the United States. Another example including when a New York cable company, Cablevision Systems Corporation, and New York-based hotel company ITT Corp. joined together in 1995 to purchase Madison Square Garden, a deal that brought with it ownership rights to the National Basketball Association's (NBA) team and the National Hockey League's (NHL) team the New York Knicks.

The major league teams that cannot or will not develop strategic alliances to tap into more revenue streams are placing themselves at a decided disadvantage to these

---

[21] "The head of the game, faced with trouble; Commissioner Fay Vincent buffeted by baseball's tough times, waves of criticism" *The Washington Post*, published August 16, 1992.

[22] "Key factors in O'Malley's decision" *The Los Angeles Times*, published January 7, 1997.

corporate machines. Historically, a world championship team is often traded the following season as proven winning players get offered top dollar from other teams. One reason for the Atlanta Braves reign as world champions in back to back years was their ability to pay the salaries to keep the team together and also trade for additional top performers to get an even stronger team.

Shared Revenue

In contrast to the cold shoulder given to the players in terms of profit sharing, the ballclub owners want to share among themselves. This practice of profit sharing among entire leagues is exemplified perfectly in the NFL. An essential factor in the success of the NFL has been its league-wide profit-sharing practices. By allowing some of the profits to go to help fund teams in smaller cities that are generating less revenue, the inferior teams can begin to pay for famous players which will help their attendance numbers. As stated previously, it is the players that the fans want to pay to watch play, not the game itself.

The idea for the MLB is to improve overall league competition, which increases the fans' interest in the league overall. It also, in time, makes pennant races closer and more games relevant later in the season. The end result is more exciting seasons for the fans and the teams. This may be good for the game of baseball, but it is a strategy that hurts the Dodgers and other major market teams like the Yankees. One report estimates the Dodgers will pay out about 5 million/year or more to other teams beginning in 1998.[23] These major changes will require the Dodgers to rethink their strategy. The ability to develop minor league talent into major league stars is a hallmark of this team. However, the economic changes could make the farm system obsolete, forcing the Dodgers to hire expensive free agent players.

Players and Coaches

Getting and keeping top performance players has become an industry money pit. With every team banking on winning seasons to fund the salaries and operating expenses, even the average players receive contract offers worth millions of dollars. The cash demands of players are eating away at the *Dodger Way*. O'Malley is being forced to raise ticket prices and broadcasting revenues just so the Dodgers can break-even. One solution for this problem, which has been heavily argued in union discussions, has been the players' willingness to settle for lower salaries if they can take part in the profit sharing. This possibility has put further pressure on the owners to concede to the union's demands.

---

[23] "Key factors in O'Malley's decision" *The Los Angeles Times*, published January 7, 1997.

As a baseball team, the 1990s proved to be a series of ups and downs for the Dodgers. The Dodgers won a division title in 1995 and a wild-card playoff berth in 1996, but it may mark the first decade since the 1930s that the ballclub will not make a World Series appearance.[24] They did have the 1996 Rookie of the Year in Hideo Nomo, but compared to the past 20 years, they are below average. Only those inside the organization really know how their minor leaguers are developing. If they cannot consistently move a couple winning players a year up to the majors, free agency practices will take all the most talented players away from the Dodgers.

In addition to the player's on-going problems, the coaching staff may need fresh talent. When Tommy Lasorda retired, Bill Russell moved up to that job. After years of being the substitute coach for Lasorda, it was unclear if Russell could show the type of leadership and fresh ideas that win close games. Yet, without a coach with the charisma of former Dodger coaching legends, this team will not be able to fulfill their potential. Proven coaches like Tommy Lasorda and Walter Alston are not easy to find and it may take Russell years to develop a personal style that wins and inspires their teams.

League Relations

Not since Bowie K. Kuhn, MLB's fifth commissioner who left office in 1984 has the Dodgers been satisfied with MLB's commissioners. MLB's commissioners are often called on to decide disputes between ballclub owners. Without a favorable commissioner and with escalating conflicts between rich and poor teams, the Dodgers cannot seem to get the support they need to make things go their way. The days when Walter O'Malley had commissioners "in his pocket" are long gone. A limited influence in ownership problems made the player's strike even more painful to Peter O'Malley, who has a great relationship with his players. His inability to get other owners to agree on a single approach to the union's demands helped the strike drag on, lacking a unified negotiating theme. "Baseball owners, in their infinite lack of wisdom, are driving O'Malley out of the game," says columnist Mike Waldner. However, Peter O'Malley has been quoted in his response as saying, "That's not a factor."[25]

Family Plans

It is unknown exactly how Walter O'Malley transferred ownership to his children without needing to liquidate a portion of it for taxes. With estate taxes as high as 55%, it is likely that he used methods permitted under 1970s tax laws which allowed certain types of trusts to transfer vast amounts without taxation. Most methods popular

---

[24] Los Angeles Dodgers Official Site. 2003 (http://losangeles.dodgers.mlb.com).

[25] "So many reasons for him to sell" *The Outlook*, published January 7, 1997.

then are no longer exempt from estate taxation. One thing is for certain, the O'Malley family must begin concerning themselves with economic and succession issues in order to have an effective strategy. At the present time, there is not an obvious successor to the Dodger legacy. Peter is aging and it seems that the time to plan for the O'Malley family future has come. A critical part of planning alternatives for the family assets is a sequence of actions which are grouped together to form sell or hold decisions. The plans must have a use of funds, if liquidated, and a way to get adequate cash out, if held. In addition, the difficult decision must be made to identify who would run the business in the future, a succession plan, and how likely conflicts can be resolved without tearing the family apart or running the team into the ground.

Alternative Investments

With the sale of the Dodger franchise, the proceeds from the sale will give the O'Malley's many alternative possible lifestyles (see Addenda 4). Certainly, a large part of the money could be invested in secure financial instruments to allow the family to enjoy much more stable returns on their investments. Any taxes due on the capital gain will be paid. With these funds, other family members would be able to pursue any projects that could never have been started due to the family's net worth being fully invested in the Dodgers.

Investments in other professional teams are also options the O'Malley's could consider. The possibility to own, as a partner, an NFL team in Los Angeles could be done with a fraction of the money (based on the values in Addenda 4). Also, as the industry changes, many other baseball teams will be up for sale. If the family bought a team in a small market, they would be able to enjoy in the money coming in from revenue sharing practices. Though Peter did not hint at any future plans in the sale announcement, it seems that the skills he has developed over a lifetime will lead him back to professional sports eventually. A certain advantage of the sale will be to let the next generation have the freedom to invest without involuntary links to other family members.

Estate and Income Taxes

The current laws provide for a 55% tax rate for estate taxes on all assets after the first 5 million and a 28% rate on income such as the proceeds from selling the Dodgers.[26] Both taxes are important and one can't choose one or the other, though some news reports[27] indicated the O'Malleys are choosing the lower income tax

---

[26] "O'My! O'Malley era ending" *The Los Angeles Times*, published January 7, 1997.

[27] "O'My! O'Malley era ending" *The Los Angeles Times*, published January 7, 1997.

instead of the higher estate tax. Usually, income tax on the capital gain is paid at the time of sale and the estate tax is based on the asset value, either the value of the team or current value of the proceeds, at the time of the owner's demise.

One advantage of not selling the team is that the actual value is debatable. By valuing the real estate and team by different methods and based on one set of assumptions or another the taxable value could vary by tens to hundreds of millions. The highest sale price of any baseball team was $173 million. This would suggest a value much lower than the $300 million plus the team may actually sell for. However, once a sale takes place, the real sale price will be the basis for estate taxes, should the sellers die near the time of the sale. It would be very difficult to get the IRS and courts to believe the sale price was irrelevant and a lower basis should be used for tax determination.

In the price range considered for the Dodgers, few conventional ways to lower estate taxes, like the $600,000 lifetime deduction, have any real impact. The assets can be transferred to a surviving spouse tax free. However, transferring property to anyone else is taxable. At the time of transfer from one generation to the next, the family will have a giant tax bill to face. This liability could require less cash out of pocket by life insurance and gifts of cash or stock, avoiding tax on the appreciation of the assets over time. However, there are not any legitimate ways to both keep control of the money and reduce estate taxes. The only good news on the estate tax front is that the IRS and courts give a reasonable time to pay taxes when the assets are illiquid and require a sale or obtaining new debt to pay, up to 15 years, payable in installments years 6–15, interest may accrue until paid in full.

The income tax due on the sale of the team will be paid in one of a few ways. One option is to pay the tax and be done with it, though it would significantly lower the net profit after tax, making the sale less financially appealing. A frequently used alternative for assets like real estate and marketable securities is to do a tax-deferred exchange on the stock sold (stock is most likely how the Dodger's ownership is held). As long as the stock is exchanged for a like investment (other stocks for example), the tax will not become payable until the stock exchanged with the initial stock is sold. This process can be repeated again and again, deferring income tax until the last trade or upon the owner's death (when the last trade occurs to liquidate the estate). Tax-deferred exchanges are great to delay tax payments, but require constant education in tax law changes to insure that all exchanges comply with IRS regulations (which change frequently). If the IRS denies the exchange as qualifying, the tax is due immediately, even if contested by the taxpayer.

Succession

This appears to be a real problem for the O'Malley's as it is for many second- and third- generation family businesses. In this case, the succession problems are in the area of operating leadership and ownership dissolution. The next president of the Dodgers will face a difficult course and cannot be successful without resources the O'Malley's do not have to invest. In addition to operating leadership, the owners also need a shared vision. As the children receive smaller percentages of the team than their parents, the needed unified decision making could be prevented if a majority with shared objectives does not form.

No one in the immediate family is ready to replace Peter, in part because no one was groomed to carry on their father's leadership role. Changes in the industry make it even more unlikely that a family member can keep the team family owned and stay competitive for very long. Without a strong leader, who has a defined vision that solves the future operations needs, a baseball franchise will never be a world champion team.

With Peter and Terry having half of the ownership and being raised in the same house, decision making was easy. However, if all owners died and each child was awarded an equal share, Peter's children will each have 16.7% and Terry's ten children would each have 5%. In addition, the children of Pete and Terry were raised in different households, which could mean different, conflicting, value systems. As the children develop their own households, the needs of various owners, such as wanting cash now from the business verses wanting future value appreciation by business growth, will be a source of conflict.

The likelihood of problems seems to grow exponentially as the number of owners grows. Communication problems become an issue in addition to the decision the communication is about. The problem of too many owners is compounded by having a few owners with over 3 times the voting power as others. Often, in situations like this, every decision becomes forced on the objecting minority by a slim majority, or the minority owners don't decide in order to hold the decision hostage until concessions are negotiated. Decision-making problems may be reduced by putting the ownership into two family trusts, but there are still too many individuals with partial control for the group to be truly effective and efficient.

Sale Results

The Dodger organization is an extension of the O'Malley family. Peter can't sell the team without concerns about the team's welfare. However, if he sees a future in which the current owners can't provide adequate capital and management vision, turning the team over to others who are more capable is a rational option. If the family receives the publicly discussed amounts of $200–500 million, the buyers must operate the business at a whopping profit to justify the investment.[28] No single family or corporation can take that much money from other profit making ventures without a plan to make a reasonable return on investment.

It is very likely that some minor league teams could be sold and Dodgertown could be spun-off as a separate professional sports facility. The biggest unknown is

---

[28] "This should be treated as a death in the family" *The Los Angeles Times*, January 7, 1997.

the team location and the stadium. Many cities would build a stadium at taxpayer expense to get the Dodgers to relocate. In fact, the same day Peter O'Malley announced that the Dodgers were for sale, Metropolitan King County Council was debating a $336 million dollar bond issue to build a new stadium for the MLB team, the Seattle Mariners.[29] The Dodger's stadium is aging and without increasing rentals, it is of limited use. The site could be used for office buildings or residential developments as a way to generate cash. However, any development plans would need approval from the same local politicians who seem difficult to appease. Another problem could be faced when trying to convince local neighborhood associations that wish to prevent additional structures on that site.[30]

Problematic Alternatives

Besides the alternatives to selling, maintaining control after succession is the main issue. Being strapped with debt could limit the family's ability to operate the team as they desire. Investment partners will require a say in decisions or at least accountability that will limit the characteristically bold moves that keeps the organization dynamic. It seems that losing total control is not very different from losing significant or majority control.

Another alternative to selling, often done in family businesses, is a transition to a professional management structure. Certainly, Walter O'Malley and the Dodger franchise have had professional management in terms of successful operations. However, the concept of professional management in family business terms implies rational decision making by persons outside the family, but on the family's behalf. The downside to this option is that professional baseball ownership is extremely labor-intensive and an absentee-owner cannot retain ownership and a credible team for very long.

A side note about the results of the sale focuses on alternative investments. Peter O'Malley has wanted a NFL team for a while.[31] If he sells the Dodgers and buys an expansion team for Los Angeles, he will encounter many of the same problems he is selling the Dodgers to escape from. The NFL has profit sharing, high player salaries, and use large stadiums which remain vacant most of the time. Another disadvantage of the NFL verses MLB is the NFL has a comparatively short season in which to generate a year's worth of revenue. However, one advantage football has is that training from high school to the pros is funded by universities. A baseball player who can't move up to the majors after a few years in the minor baseball league is a loss of a sizable investment, while a college football player who cannot succeed in profootball has no cost to the NFL franchise.

---

[29] "Baseball Economics: Selling of the dodgers - Dodgers illustrate baseball's woes - For sale sign is a chilling backdrop for M's county" *The Seattle Times*, published January 7, 1997.

[30] "Re-Imagining Dodger Stadium as urban center" *The Los Angeles Times*, January 20, 1997.

[31] "Will NFL pay dodgeball?; O'Malley wants 'sparkling, shiny, extraordinary' facility for possible new team, and he has just the place for it" *The Los Angeles Times*, published December 3, 1995.

Conclusion

As surprising as the announcement was, given the situation, the sale makes sense to Peter O'Malley. The changing business environment will require a hard-nosed management style unfamiliar to the O'Malleys. Perhaps an error of Peter was failing to develop an heir to his enterprise, groomed to succeed as an all-consumed baseball tycoon. The Dodgers investment has all of the family assets in a single, low-profit, low-liquidity investment, which is too reliant on luck. As the ownership dilutes among the third-generation children, the ability to make quick and unanimous decisions will tend to deteriorate. Even now, the decision to sell may be the only option all parties can agree on.

Personal motives are often difficult to really know. Diverse individual needs aside, this seems like a golden goose that should not be sold. Among the alternatives, a central question is the opportunity cost of the business value, and if not now, when will the time be just right, assuming that exiting the business is an eventuality.

The question of why now, and why via a press conference, are for you to ponder. Did the press conference serve notice more to the team and fans than serve an economic reason? Since the number of likely buyers who can afford investing over $150 million in a baseball team is small, is a press conference the best way to attract buyers? If the sale will take about 6 months as noted in the press conference, and the IRS gives the beneficiaries of an estate up to 10 years to pay, would selling to get cash for estate tax payments require a discount sale price? Are the tax laws soon to be less favorable for a family transfer or sale? Do the family successions needs require a decision this year and prevent training a family successor over the next 10 years? And, perhaps the most important question of all: Is there any way Peter can keep the Dodgers going the way him and his father dreamed they would always go on?

Addenda

1. Ownership Profiles as of 1985[32]
   The information below contrasts with the current ownership, which has nearly no family or single individual as the owner.

   American League

   Baltimore Orioles: Principal owner and chief executive officer is Edward Bennett Williams, a Washington, DC attorney whose other interests include a charter airline.
   Boston Red Sox: The Yawkey Foundation, whose wealth came from South Carolina real estate ventures and which retains interests in cable TV, catering, and hotels.

---

[32] "Who owns the baseball teams" *The San Francisco Chronicle*, published August 7, 1985.

California Angels: Principal owner is movie cowboy Gene Autry, whose other interests include broadcasting and hotels.

Cleveland Indians: Chairman is Patrick J. O'Neill, who has inherited extensive family interests in real estate and shipbuilding.

Chicago White Sox: Partnership led by Eddie Einhorn and Jerry Reinsdorf, who have numerous other interests, notably in real estate, cable TV, and other sports franchises.

Detroit Tigers: Owned by Tom Monaghan, founder of Domino's Pizza.

Kansas City Royals: Lead owner is Ewing Kauffman, a pharmaceuticals executive and well-known entrepreneur.

Milwaukee Brewers: Lead partner is Bud Selig, an auto distributor.

Minnesota Twins: Carl Pohlad, a Minneapolis banker.

New York Yankees: George Steinbrenner, a shipping and real estate magnate.

Oakland Athletics: The Haas family, which also owns Levi-Strauss Co.

Seattle Mariners: George Argyros, the southern California real estate developer who built Air Cal.

Texas Rangers: Jointly owned by Texas Oilman Edward Chiles and Gaylord Broadcasting Corp.

Toronto Blue Jays: Labatt Brewing Co.

National League

Atlanta Braves: Ted Turner, whose interests include other sports franchises and the TBS.

Chicago Cubs: The Tribune Co., which owns newspapers and television stations.

Cincinnati Reds: Principal owner is auto dealer Marge Schott, with a minority interest held by Multimedia Inc.

Los Angeles Dodgers: Peter O'Malley, whose late father, Walter, was a New York attorney.

Houston Astros: Principal owner is John McMullen, a New York shipbuilder and real estate developer, who acquired the team and related interests after they had been repossessed by lenders from the estate of Judge Roy Hofheinz.

Montreal Expos: Chairman is Edgar Bronfman, who also heads Seagram.

New York Mets: Nelson Doubleday, whose other interests include broadcast packaging and Doubleday Publishing Co.

Philadelphia Phillies: Bill Giles, president of the Phillies, is the son of former National League President Warren Giles and an executive with the Phillies' parent corporation, Taft Broadcasting Co.

Pittsburgh Pirates: Jointly owned by the Galbreaths, a Columbus, OH, family with extensive interests in construction, horse breeding, and Warner Communications Inc.

St. Louis cardinals: A subsidiary of Anheuser-Busch Inc., the brewing company.

San Diego Padres: Chairman is Joan Kroc, widow of McDonald's Corp. founder Ray Kroc.

San Francisco Giants: Real estate developer Robert Lurie.

2. Dodger Key Personnel, Locations and Performance

Presidents

Charles H. Byrne (1890–1897)
Charles H. Ebbets (1898–1924)
Edward J. McKeever (1925)
Wilbert Robinson (1925–1929)
Frank B. York (1930–1932)
Stephen W. McKeever (1933–1938)
Leland S. MacPhail (1938–1942)
Brach Rickey (1942–1950)
Walter O'Malley (1950–1970)
Peter O'Malley (1970 – present)

Managers Under O'Malley Family

Burt Shotton (1950)
Charlie Dressen (1951–1953)
Walter Alston (1954–1976)
Tommy Lasorda (1977–1996)
Bill Russell (1996 – present)

Team Locations

Ebbits Field, Brooklyn, NY (1914–1957)
Los Angeles Memorial Coliseum, Los Angeles, CA (1958–1961)
Dodger Stadium/Chavez Ravine, Los Angeles, CA (1962 – present)
World Championships – 1955, 1959, 1963, 1966, 1981, 1988

3. Notable Dates in Dodger History

1910 – Dodgers join MLB of the National League. New York had three teams: The New York Yankees, The Brooklyn Dodgers, and the New York Giants.

1920 – October 20, unassisted Triple play by Cleveland second baseman (only one ever in playoffs). The second baseman caught a line drive, stepped on second base before the runner could get back to the base and tagged the runner coming from first base. The Dodgers were known as "Da Bums" from their many losses.

1947 – Dodgers first play Jackie Robinson, major leagues' first black ballplayer.

1957 – Propose new stadium for Brooklyn, but city would only allow construction in Queens. This proposal was proposed as a dome stadium[33] with artificial grass, designed by Frank Lloyd Wright.

1958 – Dodgers move to Los Angeles. In a deal to make west coast games cost-effective, the New York Giants became the San Francisco Giants the same year.

1959 – Won World Series at the coliseum. This event set all-time attendance records 3 days in a row for a world series when the attendance for October 4, 5, and 6 had 92,394, 92,650, and 92,706, respectively!

1965 – Sandy Koufax pitches only perfect game in franchise's history.

1980 – Dodger stadium hosts All Star game for first time, debuts DimondVision.

1982 – Forbes Magazine called Dodgers the best managed company in sports.

1987 – Al Campanis, general manager, fired for racist remarks made on ABC's Nightline.

1988 – Fred Clair, new general manager, named executive of the year by The Sporting News.

1995 – Dodgers acquire Hideo Nomo, who becomes the first Japanese born player in major leagues.

4. Recent Sales and Value Estimates

MLB Team Sales (last 3 years)*

1994 – John Moores bought the San Diego Padres for $83 million

1994 – Peter Angelos bought the Baltimore Orioles for $173 million

1994 – Peter Magowan bought the San Francisco Giants for $100 million

1995 – 17 Person partnership bought the St. Louis Cardinals for $150 million

1995 – Steve Schott bought the Oakland A's for $50 million

1995 – Kevin McClatchy bought the Pittsburgh Pirates for $85 million

1996 – Disney bought part interest in the California Angels for $120 million

1996 – Two expansion team franchises sold for $130 million each

(*A variety of sources were used, and no details regarding what real estate and/ or minor league teams was available)

Top Five Franchises in Each Sport (estimated value in millions)**

National Basketball Assoc.	National Hockey League	National Football League	Major League Baseball
New York ($205)	Detroit ($126)	Dallas ($272)	NY Yankees ($209)
Phoenix ($191)	Chicago ($122)	Miami ($214)	Baltimore ($168)
Detroit ($185)	NY Rangers ($118)	Baltimore ($201)	Atlanta ($163)
Chicago ($178)	Boston ($111)	SF 49ers ($196)	Toronto ($152)
LA Lakers ($171)	Philadelphia ($102)	St. Louis ($193)	LA Dodgers ($147)

(**Values indicated are from a single source (Houston Mitchel, *LA Times*) and appear to be the team value without stadiums, minor league teams (if any), nor the value of ancillary revenue (related profits from profit centers feeding off the teams, i.e., TBS profits from Atlanta Braves, etc.))

---

[33] "Peter O'Malley had a tough act to follow" *The Los Angeles Times*, published January 8, 1997.

5. MLB Stadium Details[34]

National League

Team	Stadium	Yr.Blt.	Seating	Home Run Distance		
				Left	Ctr.	Right
Atlanta Braves	Alt.-Fulton Cty.	1966	52,710	335	400	330
Chicago Cubs	Wrigley Field	1914	38,765	355	400	353
Cincinnati Reds	Riverfront	1970	52,952	330	404	330
Colorado Rockies	Coors Field	1995	50,000	347	415	350
Florida Marlins	Joe Robbie	1987	48,000	335	410	345
Houston Astros	Astrodome	1965	53,821	325	400	325
L.A. Dodgers	Dodger	1962	56,000	330	395	330
Montreal Expos	Olympic	1976	46,500	325	404	325
New York Mets	Shea	1964	55,601	338	410	338
Philadelphia Phillies	Veterans	1971	62,530	330	408	330
Pittsburgh Pirates	Three Rivers	1970	47,972	335	400	335
St. Louis Cardinals	Busch	1966	57,000	330	402	330
San Diego Padres	Jack Murphy	1967	46,510	327	405	327
San Francisco	Giants Candlestick	1960	63,000	335	400	328

American League

Team	Stadium	Yr.Blt.	Seating	Home Run Distance		
				Left	Ctr.	Right
Baltimore Orioles	Camden Yards	1992	48,282	333	400	318
Boston Red Sox	Fenway Park	1912	33,871	315	420	302
California Angels	Anaheim	1966	64,593	333	404	333
Chicago White Sox	Comiskey Park	1991	44,321	347	400	347
Cleveland Indians	Jacobs Field	1994	42,400	325	405	325
Detroit Tigers	Tiger	1912	52,416	340	440	325
Kansas City Royals	Kauffman	1973	40,625	330	400	330
Milwaukee Brewers	County	1953	53,192	315	402	315
Minnesota Twins	Metrodome	1982	56,783	343	408	327
New York Yankees	Yankee	1923	57,545	312	410	310
Oakland A's	County Coliseum	1968	47,313	330	400	330
Seattle Mariners	Kingdome	1976	59,166	331	405	312
Texas Rangers	Arlington Ballpark	1994	49,292	332	400	325
Toronto Blue Jays	Skydome	1989	50,516	328	400	328

Average Stadium (both leagues) – 51,131 seats, year built on average – 1966

---

[34] *The World Almanac and book of facts – 1997*, K-III Reference Corporation Books, 1997.

6. Los Angeles Dodgers Year-by-Year Results[35]

Season	Team	League	W	L	PCT	GB	Attendance
2003	Los Angeles Dodgers	National League	85	77	0.525	15.5	3,138,626
2002	Los Angeles Dodgers	National League	92	70	0.568	6.0	3,131,255
2001	Los Angeles Dodgers	National League	86	76	0.531	6.0	3,017,143
2000	Los Angeles Dodgers	National League	86	76	0.531	11.0	3,011,539
1999	Los Angeles Dodgers	National League	77	84	0.478	22.0	3,066,588
1998	Los Angeles Dodgers	National League	83	79	0.512	15.0	3,089,201
1997	Los Angeles Dodgers	National League	88	74	0.543	2.0	3,319,504
1996	Los Angeles Dodgers	National League	90	72	0.556	1.0	3,188,454
1995	Los Angeles Dodgers	National League	78	66	0.542	–	2,766,251
1994	Los Angeles Dodgers	National League	58	56	0.509	–	2,279,355
1993	Los Angeles Dodgers	National League	81	81	0.500	23.0	3,170,392
1992	Los Angeles Dodgers	National League	63	99	0.389	35.0	2,473,266
1991	Los Angeles Dodgers	National League	93	69	0.574	1.0	3,348,170
1990	Los Angeles Dodgers	National League	86	76	0.531	5.0	3,002,396
1989	Los Angeles Dodgers	National League	77	83	0.481	14.0	2,944,653
1988	Los Angeles Dodgers	National League	94	67	0.584	–	2,980,262
1987	Los Angeles Dodgers	National League	73	89	0.451	17.0	2,797,409
1986	Los Angeles Dodgers	National League	73	89	0.451	23.0	3,023,208
1985	Los Angeles Dodgers	National League	95	67	0.586	–	3,264,593
1984	Los Angeles Dodgers	National League	79	83	0.488	13.0	3,134,824
1983	Los Angeles Dodgers	National League	91	71	0.562	–	3,510,313
1982	Los Angeles Dodgers	National League	88	74	0.543	1.0	3,608,881
1981	Los Angeles Dodgers	National League	63	47	0.573	4.0	2,381,292
1980	Los Angeles Dodgers	National League	92	71	0.564	1.0	3,249,287
1979	Los Angeles Dodgers	National League	79	83	0.488	11.5	2,860,954
1978	Los Angeles Dodgers	National League	95	67	0.586	–	3,347,845
1977	Los Angeles Dodgers	National League	98	64	0.605	–	2,955,087
1976	Los Angeles Dodgers	National League	92	70	0.568	10.0	2,386,301
1975	Los Angeles Dodgers	National League	88	74	0.543	20.0	2,539,349
1974	Los Angeles Dodgers	National League	102	60	0.630	–	2,632,474
1973	Los Angeles Dodgers	National League	95	66	0.590	3.5	2,136,192
1972	Los Angeles Dodgers	National League	85	70	0.548	10.5	1,860,858
1971	Los Angeles Dodgers	National League	89	73	0.549	1.0	2,064,594
1970	Los Angeles Dodgers	National League	87	74	0.540	14.5	1,697,142
1969	Los Angeles Dodgers	National League	85	77	0.525	8.0	1,784,527
1968	Los Angeles Dodgers	National League	76	86	0.469	21.0	1,581,093
1967	Los Angeles Dodgers	National League	73	89	0.451	28.5	1,664,362
1966	Los Angeles Dodgers	National League	95	67	0.586	–	2,617,029
1965	Los Angeles Dodgers	National League	97	65	0.599	–	2,553,577
1964	Los Angeles Dodgers	National League	80	82	0.494	13.0	2,228,751

(continued)

---

[35] Los Angeles Dodgers Official Web site. 2004 (http://losangeles.dodgers.mlb.com).

(continued)

Season	Team	League	W	L	PCT	GB	Attendance
1963	Los Angeles Dodgers	National League	99	63	0.611	–	2,538,602
1962	Los Angeles Dodgers	National League	102	63	0.618	1.0	2,755,184
1961	Los Angeles Dodgers	National League	89	65	0.578	4.0	1,804,250
1960	Los Angeles Dodgers	National League	82	72	0.532	13.0	2,253,887
1959	Los Angeles Dodgers	National League	88	68	0.564	–	2,071,045
1958	Los Angeles Dodgers	National League	71	83	0.461	21.0	1,845,556
1957	Brooklyn Dodgers	National League	84	70	0.545	11.0	1,028,258
1956	Brooklyn Dodgers	National League	93	61	0.604	–	1,213,562
1955	Brooklyn Dodgers	National League	98	55	0.641	–	1,033,589
1954	Brooklyn Dodgers	National League	92	62	0.597	5.0	1,020,531
1953	Brooklyn Dodgers	National League	105	49	0.682	–	1,163,419
1952	Brooklyn Dodgers	National League	96	57	0.627	–	1,088,704
1951	Brooklyn Dodgers	National League	97	60	0.618	1.0	1,282,628
1950	Brooklyn Dodgers	National League	89	65	0.578	2.0	1,185,896
1949	Brooklyn Dodgers	National League	97	57	0.630	–	1,633,747
1948	Brooklyn Dodgers	National League	84	70	0.545	7.5	1,398,967
1947	Brooklyn Dodgers	National League	94	60	0.610	–	1,807,526
1946	Brooklyn Dodgers	National League	96	60	0.615	2.0	1,796,824
1945	Brooklyn Dodgers	National League	87	67	0.565	11.0	1,059,220
1944	Brooklyn Dodgers	National League	63	91	0.409	42.0	605,905
1943	Brooklyn Dodgers	National League	81	72	0.529	23.5	661,739
1942	Brooklyn Dodgers	National League	104	50	0.675	2.0	1,037,765
1941	Brooklyn Dodgers	National League	100	54	0.649	–	1,214,910
1940	Brooklyn Dodgers	National League	88	65	0.575	12.0	975,978
1939	Brooklyn Dodgers	National League	84	69	0.549	12.5	955,668
1938	Brooklyn Dodgers	National League	69	80	0.463	18.5	663,087
1937	Brooklyn Dodgers	National League	62	91	0.405	33.5	482,481
1936	Brooklyn Dodgers	National League	67	87	0.435	25.0	489,618
1935	Brooklyn Dodgers	National League	70	83	0.458	29.5	470,517
1934	Brooklyn Dodgers	National League	71	81	0.467	23.5	434,188
1933	Brooklyn Dodgers	National League	65	88	0.425	26.5	526,815
1932	Brooklyn Dodgers	National League	81	73	0.526	9.0	681,827
1931	Brooklyn Dodgers	National League	79	73	0.520	21.0	753,133
1930	Brooklyn Dodgers	National League	86	68	0.558	6.0	1,097,329
1929	Brooklyn Dodgers	National League	70	83	0.458	28.5	731,886
1928	Brooklyn Dodgers	National League	77	76	0.503	17.5	664,863
1927	Brooklyn Dodgers	National League	65	88	0.425	28.5	637,230
1926	Brooklyn Dodgers	National League	71	82	0.464	17.5	650,819
1925	Brooklyn Dodgers	National League	68	85	0.444	27.0	659,435
1924	Brooklyn Dodgers	National League	92	62	0.597	1.5	818,883
1923	Brooklyn Dodgers	National League	76	78	0.494	19.5	564,666
1922	Brooklyn Dodgers	National League	76	78	0.494	17.0	498,865
1921	Brooklyn Dodgers	National League	77	75	0.507	16.5	613,245
1920	Brooklyn Dodgers	National League	93	61	0.604	–	808,722
1919	Brooklyn Dodgers	National League	69	71	0.493	27.0	360,721
1918	Brooklyn Dodgers	National League	57	69	0.452	25.5	83,831
1917	Brooklyn Dodgers	National League	70	81	0.464	26.5	221,619

(continued)

(continued)

Season	Team	League	W	L	PCT	GB	Attendance
1916	Brooklyn Dodgers	National League	94	60	0.610	–	447,747
1915	Brooklyn Dodgers	National League	80	72	0.526	10.0	297,766
1914	Brooklyn Dodgers	National League	75	79	0.487	19.5	122,671
1913	Brooklyn Dodgers	National League	65	84	0.436	34.5	347,000
1912	Brooklyn Dodgers	National League	58	95	0.379	46.0	243,000
1911	Brooklyn Dodgers	National League	64	86	0.427	33.5	269,000
1910	Brooklyn Dodgers	National League	64	90	0.416	40.0	279,321
1909	Brooklyn Dodgers	National League	55	98	0.359	55.5	321,300
1908	Brooklyn Dodgers	National League	53	101	0.344	46.0	275,600
1907	Brooklyn Dodgers	National League	65	83	0.439	40.0	312,500
1906	Brooklyn Dodgers	National League	66	86	0.434	50.0	277,400
1905	Brooklyn Dodgers	National League	48	104	0.316	56.5	227,924
1904	Brooklyn Dodgers	National League	56	97	0.366	50.0	214,600
1903	Brooklyn Dodgers	National League	70	66	0.515	19.0	224,670
1902	Brooklyn Dodgers	National League	75	63	0.543	27.5	199,868
1901	Brooklyn Dodgers	National League	79	57	0.581	9.5	198,200
1900	Brooklyn Dodgers	National League	82	54	0.603	–	170,000
1899	Brooklyn Dodgers	National League	101	47	0.682	–	269,641
1898	Brooklyn Dodgers	National League	54	91	0.372	46.0	122,514
1897	Brooklyn Dodgers	National League	61	71	0.462	32.0	220,831
1896	Brooklyn Dodgers	National League	58	73	0.443	33.0	201,000
1895	Brooklyn Dodgers	National League	71	60	0.542	16.5	230,000
1894	Brooklyn Dodgers	National League	70	61	0.534	20.5	214,000
1893	Brooklyn Dodgers	National League	65	63	0.508	20.5	235,000
1892	Brooklyn Dodgers	National League	95	59	0.617	9.0	183,727
1891	Brooklyn Dodgers	National League	61	76	0.445	25.5	181,477
1890	Brooklyn Dodgers	National League	86	43	0.667	–	121,412
1889	Brooklyn Dodgers	American Association	93	44	0.679	–	353,690
1888	Brooklyn Dodgers	American Association	88	52	0.629	6.5	245,000
1887	Brooklyn Dodgers	American Association	60	74	0.448	34.5	273,000
1886	Brooklyn Dodgers	American Association	76	61	0.555	16.0	185,000
1885	Brooklyn Dodgers	American Association	53	59	0.473	26.0	85,000
1884	Brooklyn Dodgers	American Association	40	64	0.385	33.5	65,000

Learning Notes

Reasons to sell now

1. Capital requirements. If the organization needed millions of dollars, the family either would not have it or would not want the problem of paying back a debt from limited profits. Looking for debt funding or partners when in a cash crisis can force the family to give too much to keep team. Yearly needs of high player salaries, major repairs to the stadium, launching an international marketing effort for increased broadcasting revenue, or just keeping up with what other teams have could generate a cash crisis.

(continued)

2. Top price today ($300–500 million). Tomorrow may see a possible decline from team performance woes or more strikes; in 1995, Dodgers ended in the red. Possible loss of income from a union strike is 5 years away, but could lower the value as the contract nears expiration (see Addenda 4 for recent sales).
3. Better Opportunity. Does Peter know what to do with the sale proceeds? Does he have plans to purchase another sports team or other assets? No point in selling if you can't reinvest into a better situation!
4. Replacing Tommy Lasorda and other key personnel. Any replacement will be taking a chance. The possibility of the team losing for years before a new coach is able to prove himself is a problem. Replacing Bill Russell would be very expensive. The farm system so well known for outstanding players has not been as successful in growing coaches (many are famous Dodger players of the past or have been with the organization forever). Peter can look toward the farm system and fail to identify significant stars of tomorrow. Free agents have a history of high costs and poor performance with the Dodgers.
5. Union Trouble. All contracts short term, problems ahead verses marketing expertise of the National Basketball Association, National Football, and of course, the National Hockey League (in addition to hundreds of others).
6. City Trouble. Can't get the football team and stadium to expand family business, city could prevent attempts to use land for offices, residential, etc.
7. Succession Issues. There are five major factors of successful succession in the opinion of many consultants. These may not have been addressed or even approached by Peter in terms of his children. How well were they addressed by Peter and Walter is another issue to address.
8. Ownership Training. It is unclear how much Peter wanted to become president of the Dodgers, and how much Walter influenced this decision. Walter was very overbearing, and it seems that Peter was groomed to take over.

Alternatives to selling and related issues

1. Unlimited spousal transfer – if Annette outlives Peter, give his part to her without tax.
2. Insurance – life insurance is a way to spend less today for more at time of death. This could provide the cash needed for taxes.
3. Delay tax payment – the IRS gives closely held business owners up to 10 years to pay estate taxes. Certainly, if Peter could sell the team in 6 months, his children could manage to sell the team in 10 years.
4. Purchase sister's shares – a buyout of Terry at least keeps the team in the family. This purchase could be done with debt or preferred stock (without voting rights). This would avoid diluting ownership.
5. Tax loopholes – Though this much capital gain requires some taxes, exceptions like IRS Code 6166 differs up to a million dollars and IRS Code 2032a

(continued)

provides an argument that the property's value is based on current use and not the highest and best use (lowering the taxable value). Each method has restrictions and maximum amounts, but all need to be explored.

6. Alternative sale methods – Techniques like tax-deferred exchanges and installment sales are possible. In a tax-deferred exchange, no gain is realized if exchanged for like property. This would allow diversification of Dodger stock into other stocks.

7. Gifts – though the tax free limit is $10,000/person/year, even paying tax allows all future appreciation to get to the heirs and escapes estate tax.

8. Irrevocable Trusts – though an arcane part of the law, if each owner set up a trust for the children, then the results would retain 50% ownership by each trust. To further protect the family, the trustees could include a giant trust company and a separate company owned by the children with the expressed authority to replace the corporate trustee, insuring family control.

Peter's way[36]

Beyond all the pleasures and problems of ownership, the decision to sell ultimately was a personal statement. Peter needs to do things his way, or not at all. If he could, he would repeat the 1988 season forever. That was the last World Champion Dodger team and was at a time when few of the current rashes of changes and strategic issues were little more than hypothetical.

Peter has a style that has been developed for a lifetime and has been remarkably successful. Its hard to imagine Peter, or anyone in the family, being able to succeed in baseball as a family business, with the direction the industry is going. The days of free spending on the team and low ticket prices are more in the past than the future. It may be difficult to see how the O'Malleys can change with the times while retain their style. If Peter could see a way to have a family member have the freedom he has enjoyed and the Dodgers remain a competitive team, it is questionable that this team would even be for sale today. In addition to the pressures of competing with corporate owners, the needs of the family must be given more weight than the team's needs. This is the only team whose owner has no other or bigger investments. Modern portfolio theory would suggest that diversification is essential for a family with assets worth over a hundred million dollars. To see the stock market, set one record high after another, yet keeping all your money in a sports team with low income and high risk is foolish. Losing full ownership will get some cash out of the business, but can't solve the future organization needs for growth and reserves. By selling only a small part now, the need to sell larger parts of the franchise later becomes inevitable. In many ways, the family's past success in baseball has limited its future options.

---

[36] This is the case authors' opinion, based on the research completed, but is not fact.

Chapter 7
Case Five: The Vicente Family and Their Santa Maria Store – Small Business Growth and Succession in Puerto Rico

This case was researched and developed by Alex Galindo and was written under the supervision of Alan Carsrud and Malin Brännback. The names in this case have been changed, but the facts presented are based on a real family firm in Puerto Rico. This case examines the transition of an entrepreneurial firm to a family-owned one. It discusses the issues of what happens when there is planning for starting a firm and later having family involvement in the firm.

The Early Years

In 1965, Antonio Vicente de Toro had an idea to open a business that 40 years later was perceived as brilliant by most of his friends and family. However, initially his friends and especially his wife thought Antonio was crazy. His new wife, Alicia, was heard to say that a liquor store was a waste of their limited resources and Antonio needed to get a real job to support her and the children they hoped to have. While working within retailing was acceptable to his family, Antonio was focused on one very particular type of retail establishment. He did not just want to work in a store, he wanted to sell liquor and spirits and own the store. This idea became his passion and the intent to start a store morphed into a reality.

However, his parents, Jorge and Elina wanted their oldest son to migrate to New York City to take advantage of what they saw as the best place for any young Puerto Rican male to find a real job: working for a large firm. Then he could send money back to support them. They saw Antonio in New York as becoming the foundation for a new life for his siblings far away from Puerto Rico.

Nevertheless, working for someone else was not in Antonio's DNA. Despite the negative feedback of his friends and family, Antonio took his meager savings and opened a small liquor store on a busy street corner in downtown Mayaguez, Puerto Rico, which he named for his patron saint, Santa Maria. In 1965, there were only two other liquor stores in Puerto Rico, both located in the capital city of San Juan.

A.L. Carsrud and M. Brännback, *Family Firms in Transition: Case Studies on Succession, Inheritance, and Governance*, SpringerBriefs in Business 3, DOI 10.1007/978-1-4614-1201-4_7, © Alan L. Carsrud and Malin Brännback, 2011

The city of Mayaguez is in the western part of the island and his liquor store was thus the only one for miles around. Antonio realized there were a lot of people in his area of the island who did not want to go to San Juan every time they needed to buy distilled spirits for their personal use, to sell in their restaurants, or serve in local bars. Antonio felt that being physically close to their businesses and a member of the local community should bring him a lot of clients.

Lacking a business education, and not knowing what business plans or market analyses were, he just paid attention to what he saw around him. It was this attention to the need of people around him and what they say they wanted that gave Antonio an idea. As a young man, he used to frequently visit bars in Mayaquez with his male friends on weekends. He soon realized that he could be the supplier to those bars. The idea, to him, was great. He would say in later years "… this was easy, I already knew everybody that had bars around my area, so it was not difficult to have the bars as customers." Santa Maria started out being the main, and for a long time, the only supplier of alcohol to the western part of the island. Ultimately, the Vicente family would realize that this was going to be a business that could last for a long time. This realization, however, did not come quickly and it did bring strain to the family; Antonio needed to grow the business and, ultimately, help in running the business.

Work Had To Be Done

After opening Santa Maria, Antonio began to realize that he needed to bring more clients. To do this, he needed to market his store. But he would have to do this all by himself as he had no employees. Even though, he had already some client bars, those customers alone were not going to support his family or keep the store open. He soon realized that he had to create a clientele plus be the supplier of those clients. After a year of the store opening, and with his wife, Alicia, pregnant with their second child, he made the decision that to succeed he was going to have to grow his market and not only run a liquor store, but deliver the products he sold and marketing his services to more bars around the North West and South West regions of the island.

In some ways, Antonio was becoming a distributor, although he never used that term and simply saw himself as selling the various brands he carried in the store directly to local bars and restaurants without them having to come to his store. Antonio decided to go to the different bars or any local grocery that sold alcohol and tell them about his business. At the beginning, this was very hard because at that time there were not that many bars close by and most of those already were clients of his. Delivery became an important part of his "business to business strategy" because his clients saw that as something of value to them. Otherwise, they would have to drive for over an hour to San Juan to pick up liquor for their bars.

Antonio did this direct marketing of his store the same way for 10 years. "I did it this way because that was the only way I knew how to do it. I did not know anything about marketing nor did I learn this in school." In 1965, in Puerto Rico there were not many media channels that you could use to let people know what you were selling. "La Ruta" was the route that he had to take every single day to supply his various clients around the western third of Puerto Rico and to locate and visit potential new customers. By the eighth year of operation, this marketing/delivery operation took up to 5 h every day. This routine was very difficult for him because he need to be in the store as well as deliver. It became clear that Antonio need his wife to work for him at the store location in Mayaguez.

When Business Becomes a Family Firm

Alicia, his wife, had been a secretary to a heart doctor in Mayaguez for 2 years when she met Antonio one Saturday night. She was out dancing with a group of her girl-friends at a local bar when this tall young man with wavy hair walked into the bar. She fell in love with Antonio almost instantly with his good looks and passion for life. Once they married she continued to work for the doctor as she was not sure Antonio could make sufficient money to support their growing family. The doctor allowed her flexibility in her work hours so she could take care of their first born child, Pito, when her mother and/or mother-in-law could not take care of him. When Antonio asked her to work in the store she had been working for the doctor for almost 10 years and she and Antonio had two children. She saw her job as the steady income the family needed and besides she knew nothing about liquors or retail sales. When Antonio asked her to work with him at the liquor store she obviously balked. But she understood that her husband needed her support at the store. Besides she hated to see her husband working 16 hour days.

Before leaving her previous job, she really had to think seriously about joining her husband in a business that was male dominated. At that time, women were not treated the same way as now in the business world. Alicia had a relative high paying job and it was a tough decision to leave the doctor's office. She understood that she was going to be at the store by herself and that if something happened she did not had Antonio to help her. This made it even tougher for her to quit her secure job. After all this internal debate, she decided to work for Antonio and help him grow the business. She would say later to friends that "…I did not have any other choice but to work at the store and help my husband grow his business." From 1965 to the early 1970s, she was his only employee, although she never saw a paycheck. Despite the fact that their family income initially dropped when she quit her job to work in the store, Alicia took it as a challenge. She began to see a future in what Antonio was doing.

Initially working in the store was a shock. Alicia had to take care of the store while taking orders that came in by phone or through the door. She did not know all of the names of the beers, rum, etc., so at the beginning it was very difficult. If some-body went to the store and wanted something she had to take care of it. This is when trouble began. Some of their customers where not nice to her at times and a few men tried to sexually touch her. When she did not know what something was or where something is, some would verbally abused her. When Antonio found out he would drop that client instantly and make them drive to San Juan for their liquor. Once he actually knocked down a client in a fight who was trying to make advances toward Alicia and kicked him out of the store. The harassment stopped after word got around the community that Antonio had a "…mean right arm."

She later would tell her daughter-in-law that these were the worst years of her life and that it took her almost a year to understand everything about the business and learn to deal with some of the less desirable clients they had. After several years, she became very good at her job. Antonio would later say "…they respected her more than me and several thought of the business as hers." Alicia also began to think of the business as much hers as Antonio's.

Growing the Business

With the help of Alicia, Antonio was able to grow the business to the point where they needed to make decision about the store's location and future growth. After 5 years of struggle, Santa Maria became one of the major suppliers of alcohol products in Puerto Rico. In 1970, Antonio made a decision that today he does not regret, but then nearly made them sell their home and borrow heavily from a local bank. Alicia worried that this was going to mean the loss of their home. Antonio knew this decision was difficult because his clients were starting to worry if he could serve them adequately. The initial store location was becoming too small for the demand he was generating from his clients. He had to make a decision quickly. He needed a warehouse that could hold the entire inventory while not impacting the store operations. Before they bought the new location, Santa Maria looked a mess with all the beers, rum, etc. stored everywhere because of the limited space available. This did not give clients a good impression of the store. So he decided to move the store to a new location.

In May, 1970, he bought a place across the street from the store and moved Santa Maria there. This helped him convert the old store into a warehouse, and now he could bring more products there and expand his commercial business. This decision was very successful because around the time that it was made, the demand for alcohol increased tremendously because resorts where being build nearby as well as more vacation homes near the beaches. He and Alicia decided to hire two employees. This was very tough for them because he now needed to pay people to work for him. Alicia was happy as she would have company in the store. Antonio, the great risk taker, was wondering if he should take the risk of hiring. Alicia thought otherwise and at her urging, he decided to hire. One would stay with Alicia at the store and the other one would go with him to do the route.

More Growth

Antonio, while doing his daily route, thought of something additional that helped the business keep growing: another store. This new location opened in 1976 in Yauco, PR. The idea of another store started because he realized that at that there was only one highway that leads to the capital, San Juan. This highway passed through downtown Yauco, and he soon realized that Santa Maria could be successful in Yauco. But the opening of this store created another problem. Who was going to manage the Yauco store? Alicia and Antonio talked about it and determined that Antonio was going to work out of Yauco and Alicia was going to work in Mayaguez, the main store. They felt this was the easiest solution as Alicia already had the experience working at the Mayaguez store, knew those customers, and she could stay close to home and the children.

The Yauco store was very successful for almost 5 years. Then Antonio realized that something was going to happen that would require he change the business again. At the time they opened the Yauco store, the commonwealth government began to build a new highway that went from Mayaguez directly to San Juan, by passing Yauco. As with all government projects in Puerto Rico, Antonio thought he would be long retired before the highway bypass was completed. However, before opening the store he knew about this construction and he was prepared to make decisions if and when they ever finished the new highway. A year before they opened the new highway, he made the decision to close the store and sell that location. He understood that traffic was not going to pass through downtown Yauco anymore and that the demand for the store was going to diminish significantly. This was a very important decision as he would later tell his son "… if I would have kept that store opened, I would have lost money and your mother would not have been happy with me." As it turned out, he did not lose on the sale and had sufficient profits from the real estate sale to do other things, like open another store.

In 1981, after closing the Yauco store Antonio and Alicia decided to open another store; in this case a second store in Mayaguez. This new store would take a different approach to selling than the others. Since he frequently visited the local Farmer's Market, he saw the possibility of customer demand if he opened a store there. This new store, however, had a different concept than the other ones, the concept of cash and carry. He wanted to sell at near wholesale prices to regular retail customers, not just wholesale to bars and clubs. This store was very successful because there was no such concept in liquors stores at that time in Mayaguez. The original Santa Maria Store in Mayaguez had been doing primarily a wholesale business, but Antonio was thinking about the future and depending primarily on wholesale business to bars and clubs was not in the plans. He wanted to build a new main store and make a top notch retail and wholesale liquor store. At this time, he also began to think that his son, Pito, should take over the family business in the near future. However, he never really discussed this "plan" with his wife or son.

Crisis in the Family

In 1988, there was a new problem facing the family and the business. Antonio Vicente had not been feeling quite his usual energetic self for quite a while. His wife kept urging him to go to the doctor to find out what was wrong. One morning Antonio finally went to the doctor because his legs were hurting. It was the same doctor that Alicia had worked for many years before. After a long wait and a lot of tests, Dr. Francisco Gomez told him that he had poor circulation in his legs and that soon or later if he kept working the way he was, he would not be able to walk again. This was very hard news to take for both Antonio and the family. It was totally unexpected. Even though Pito was more involved in the store, Antonio thought he was not ready to take over. Alicia, on the other hand, was worried that Antonio might die and she wanted him to quit the business immediately and turn it over to Pito. Antonio did not know what to do. Antonio asked the doctor if he eased up on the daily activities would he be able to work until his son was ready to take over. Dr. Gomez said yes and Antonio was back on his feet working and making the store better. This, however, did not make Alicia happy, but only caused her more worry about the man she loved.

More Unfortunate Things Happen

In late November, 1988, another unfortunate thing occurred. Late on a Sunday evening, the Vicente family received a call that changed the business drastically. A friend of the family was driving through the commercial district where the Santa Maria Warehouse was located. It was on fire. The entire family rushed to the warehouse; what they saw was not good. The whole building was on fire. This fire cost them over a million dollars. The building was 75% burned and the inventory was 85% lost. Antonio only had the retail operation which he closed for 2 months, so he could use the space to try to reestablish his wholesale distribution business which still accounted for 70% if their revenues. This meant they lost revenues from their cash and carry retail.

The fire was very hard emotionally on Antonio and Alicia because the original warehouse location for Santa Maria meant so much to the Vicente family. Antonio now had to make another decision, should they rebuild the warehouse or should they try to open in a new location. Antonio and his family decided that what is best for the warehouse to stay in the original location because everybody knew where they are located. He also thought that by rebuilding the warehouse, it would mean more to the family and to their community. This news was big in the city of Mayaguez as it meant the warehouse jobs would not be lost to another city. The local Chamber of Commerce helped arrange for a bank loan and the city government provided dump trucks to take away the remains of the burned out building. Antonio could not believe how people were trying to help them. It was the support from a big supplier that surprised him most, however.

At the current time, none of his nephews or nieces work in the firm and none have expressed an interest in being involved in the business. Pito thinks this may be because his mother tells her grandchildren what a hard life it was in the family business. His brother and sister still provide professional services to the firm when he needs their expertise.

This lack of planning for the future both in terms of growth and succession should be of concern, but Pito does not want to face the fact he might die like his father and has even been heard to joke "... if I don't have a last testament then I won't die." While he agrees with his siblings and mother that Santa Maria is successful now, he worries what would happen if another fire occurs? Yet he does not seem to want to answer the questions of What happens if something happens to him? Who will take over the store? All Pito will say to his family and friends is that he wants to keep the store open until he cannot deal with it anymore. Pito may have planned the wine cava in Santa Maria, but planning on succession and ownership inheritance does not seem to be high on his list of priorities.

Pito has recently been dating a beautiful young widow, Maria, who is 33 with three very young sons. What if Pito marries Maria, who will inherit the half of the firm he owns? To whom will his aging mother leave her half ownership? If Pito marries Maria, how is he going to deal with young children who are not biologically his? Antonio did a fine job raising him and incorporating him in the business, but Pito seemingly is less willing to engage his nephews and nieces in the firm. Would he act the same way with his step-children? The future of Santa Maria is unclear.

Time Line

1965 – Antonio Vicente founded the Santa Maria Liquor Store.
1970 – Expand the original store to have more space for inventory.
1976 – Open a second store in Yauco, PR.
1981 – Closed Yauco store due to a new highway.
1981 – Opens another store in the Farmer's Market in Mayaguez.
1982 – "Pito" started to be more involve in the store.
1984 – Antonio expands the original store and moves Farmer's Market store to a bigger location.
1988 – Antonio was diagnosed heart trouble and bad circulation.
1988 – The original warehouse store catches fire.
1990 – 25th Anniversary ceremony.
1990 – Antonio "Pito" Vicente Jr. takes over the store.
1992 – Pito opens a wine cava and Antonio Sr. dies.
1993 – Pito expands wine cava with fine wines from Spain, California, and South America.

The Players

Antonio Vicente, the founder of the Santa Maria Liquor Store. He worked the business for 23 years before retiring in 1988, due to bad circulation in his legs. Antonio took up the "cock fighting business" and died in 1992.

Alicia Rivera, 70 – wife of Antonio Vicente. She was a secretary of a major doctor's office in Mayaguez before joining the business. She is now retired, owns 50% of Santa Maria, but is not involved in the business. She was head of the marketing department, and until her husband's death, went by the stores often to check on them.

Antonio "Pito" Vicente, 44 – oldest of three siblings. Has a degree in Finance and Management from the University of Mayaguez – Puerto Rico. In 1990, he took over the store and successfully made it better. He opened the wine cellar to give the store a different outlook, still 50% owner of the store now. He is unmarried but dating a widow with three sons.

Samuel Vicente, 43 – has a degree in Accounting. He started working at the store when he was 7 years old. But as time went by, his desire to work there diminish. He is involved only in the financial aspect of the store. He is married with four children, two boys and two girls.

Marlene Vicente, 38 – youngest of three siblings and the only daughter of Antonio and Alicia. She has a master's degree in Psychology and now is working on her doctoral degree. She works for the Inter American University where her husband is a professor. They have three daughters. She was never involved in the company.

Learning Notes

1. What would you do to market the store when it started?
2. Would you do what Antonio did to start and grow his business?
3. If you were Alicia, would you have quit your job and go work for Antonio?
4. Should Alicia have kept working at the store even though all the harassment she was receiving?
5. What should have Antonio done when the doctor first told him about his poor blood circulation?
6. Do you agree with the way Antonio handled the succession and ownership of the firm?
7. What would have happened to the business if Pito was not experience or educated?
8. Did Pito do the right thing of introducing the cava to the store?
9. What kind of succession planning should Pito do?

Chapter 8
Case Six: Jacoby Construction, Inc. – Building a Strong Family Firm on the Sound Foundation of Succession

Introduction

This case was developed by Mark Gardhouse and Alan Carsrud. The names and some of the persons in the case have been changed at the request of the firm. This case is an example of how succession properly handled can provide for the long-term viability of the firm as it transitions through various succession cycles.

History, Challenge, and Firm Overview

Jacoby and Sons, Inc. ("Jacoby" or the "Company") builds foundations for infrastructure projects and designs and manufactures speciality equipment for the foundation construction market. The Company, based in Toronto, Ontario, Canada, provides foundation solutions for bridges/ports, hospitals, airports, water/waste treatment, and commercial/residential developments. Since its inception over 100 years ago, the Company has been a pioneer in developing and implementing new foundation technologies.

The Company was founded in Canada in 1897 by Thomas Jacoby, the great grandfather of Patrick Jacoby, the present CEO, and has remained a family business and community leader since that time. Jacoby Foundation has been known as a pioneer in developing and implementing new foundation technologies all around the world. It also has a long history of inventing solutions to foundation challenges and is well recognized in its use of ingenuity to solve problems that other firms cannot.

The Company has developed into two divisions: (1) *Construction* – provides pile driving and related services to the construction industry, utilizing their own products, and (2) *Manufacturing* – designs and builds large tools for the pile driving and foundation industry. The Company's products and services are sold worldwide.

As Patrick Jacoby, the current CEO reflects on the Company's successes, he knows he needs to seek growth capital which will allow the firm to increase working

A.L. Carsrud and M. Brännback, *Family Firms in Transition: Case Studies on Succession, Inheritance, and Governance*, SpringerBriefs in Business 3, DOI 10.1007/978-1-4614-1201-4_8, © Alan L. Carsrud and Malin Brännback, 2011

capital, expand the equipment rental/leasing program, and acquire an industry-related business. Patrick is concerned about what type of structure would be best for the company, how much control is he prepared to relinquish to a new partner, and who and where should he look for the growth capital. He is not sure how to go about this challenge and what the outcome will be.

Company Divisional Overview

Jacoby Construction (66% of revenue): the construction division provides foundation construction work to a variety of industries. Jacoby Construction personnel and equipment are currently working on 22 different projects across Canada and other parts of the world, including work on the foundation for the Humber Bridge on the QEW, industrial work in the Athabasca oil sands, and cofferdams for the Sir Adam Beck hydroelectric mega-project in Niagara Falls.

Jacoby Manufacturing (33% of revenue): the manufacturing division designs and builds specialty pile-driving hammers, vertical travel leads, drills, and testing equipment for the foundation industry, employing its own patented designs for sale domestically and for export to over 40 countries. Technology and innovation are cornerstones to the design of each of its tools. In addition to manufacturing specialty equipment, Jacoby has started a rental program for its specialty equipment. Frequently, a rental order often turns into a purchase order. Jacoby Construction and Jacoby Manufacturing's respective activities are highly synergistic. The combination of hands-on experience in the field and innovation in the design and manufacturing areas constitutes key sustainable competitive advantages.

Key Management

The Company is led by a member of the founding family, Patrick Jacoby, age 52, who is CEO. He has been responsible for the recent expansion of the Company's business and who has also been responsible for many industry-leading equipment design innovations. As the great grandson of the founder, he is the main creative force and visionary behind its success and also has responsibility for a number of the Company's larger accounts, including numerous international accounts. Peter is married with two very young daughters and has decided that he would like to have the employees of the firm ultimately end up with the ownership of the firm via an employee stock ownership plan. This would allow him to exit the firm with substantial wealth.

Peter Smyth-Jones, a civil engineer, currently Vice-President of both the manufacturing and construction operations, was hired in 2003. He has been responsible for the day-to-day operations of the Company since 2007. With the potential growth capital in place, Patrick Jacoby is thinking of moving Peter to the President position as a part of the succession transition he wants to put into place. Peter currently owns a small portion of the firm's stock as a key employee.

The Company's VP Finance, Teddy Taylor is an experienced intermediate accountant; however, given the Company's projected growth, the Company is currently undertaking a process to hire an experienced CFO. Other key operating staff members have been recently added in manufacturing and operations.

The Company, Revenue, and Ownership Structure

Jacoby operates under the market name of "Jacoby Solutions" with two operating divisions: Jacoby Construction and a manufacturing division called Jacoby Manufacturing. The construction division provides foundation construction work to a variety of industries, predominantly in southern Ontario. Historically, Jacoby has primarily acted as a subcontractor to the main project operator, though increasingly they are participating in or leading design-build consortiums to jointly bid on contracts. Jacoby's sustainable competitive advantage currently stems from the synergies of its construction experience combined with innovative equipment development. The Company has developed many patented technologies, widely used in the global foundation industry.

Over the next 5 years, Jacoby plans to increase its revenues from the current level of $37–70 million per annum with a corresponding improvement in profitability. The Company intends to further enhance its unique synergy of construction and manufacturing as part of this growth program. Patrick Jacoby also wants to make several strategic acquisitions and investments. The firm's core strategy is to leverage its specialization in foundation construction to become the industry leader, both domestically and internationally. The Company plans to expand its variety of technologies and services it offers, including manufacturing, leasing equipment, engineering services, and foundation testing.

The Company is presently owned 95% by Patrick Jacoby. Over a half century ago, Patrick's grandfather passed on all ownership shares to Patrick's father, Thomas. In turn, at the appropriate time, Thomas transferred all ownership shares to Patrick and set up life insurance policies for his one brother and sisters as their equivalent compensation. In 1996, Patrick began a program where senior management could buy a small number of shares of the company.

Jacoby Manufacturing Division

The Jacoby Manufacturing Division designs and manufactures foundation equipment, and has been an innovator in developing specialized tools and solutions for the foundation industry. During the 1960s, the Company experimented with improvements to the construction equipment it used for foundation work. This led to the creation of this division in 1969. The symbiotic relationship between the two divisions is such that the construction division provides much of the initial research and development work, while the manufacturing division provides specialized equipment and a competitive advantage to the construction division. This includes clean burning hammers, vertical travel leads, and Statnamic load testing

Pile Driving Hammers

Jacoby is the only North American producer of diesel pile driving hammers, which account for some 60% of the division's total revenue. Jacoby is also the world's only producer of clean burning diesel hammers. These environmentally friendly hammers are becoming increasingly sought after, as regulators insist on clean burning equipment near waterways and the US Environmental Protection Agency is in the process of implementing regulations to clean up diesel emission in the construction industry. The Company has a wide range of sizes of clean hammers with six models available and development of a seventh underway. Jacoby's product range is able to meet the requirements for 90% of the demand of the on-shore foundation market.

In 2004, Jacoby signed a multiyear contract with the US Army to manufacture a large number of pile drivers for building temporary bridges to move troops in the field. Jacoby was the only manufacturer able to meet the US Army's strict equipment requirements. The project, which has just delivered its last hammer, contributed a substantial gross margin on the business. This programme has well positioned the Company to supply other arms of the US military and NATO forces with similar equipment.

Equipment Rental

In recent years, Jacoby has built and acquired a small fleet of foundation equipment for rent to general contractors and other foundation companies. The fleet includes 15 hammers, vertical travel leads, cranes, and drilling equipment. The equipment is normally rented on a percentage value of the market price of the equipment and varies (on average) between 3 and 8% of the value (charged per month), which indicates a payback period of 13–36 months. The expected life of equipment within the rental pool is 10–25 years. The rental business has grown strongly from $500,000 in 2004 to $1.3 million in 2006. Market demand for rental equipment comes from customers who buy specialized equipment for specific products, only to end up selling the asset after the job is done. General contractors don't like to have cash tied up in equipment and a rental option provides a method to reduce overall capital invested. Equipment rental has very high returns +40% gross margins. Historically, however, much of the equipment was financed by operating leases (predominantly with GE Capital).

By 2003, Jacoby's existing bank advances and long-term loans precluded it from accessing further bank financing, so they utilized "off balance sheet" financing. Over the past 4 years, the Company has manufactured over $6 million of rental equipment assets that are not directly reflected on Jacoby's balance sheet (via operating leases from GE Capital).

Jacoby Construction Division

Jacoby Construction provides foundation construction work to a variety of industries, predominantly in Ontario; however, the company is increasing its geographic footprint across Canada and the US with projects in the oil sands in Alberta and in Vancouver for the 2010 Olympics. Historically, Jacoby has primarily acted as a subcontractor to the main project operator, though increasingly they are participating in or leading design-build consortiums to jointly bid on contracts. Jacoby's work is well diversified into four primary market segments, comprising transportation, municipal, residential, and industrial. Historically, transportation has accounted for some 40–60% of total revenue, municipal 15–30%, and the residential and industrial markets make up the balance.

The Company's business can also be categorized by foundation type, including (1) displacement piles, (2) nondisplacement piles, and (3) shoring/marine work, with an almost equal split between each category on average. Displacement piling involves prefabricated piles (typically steel or concrete), which are driven into the ground using a pile driver (or hammer) to provide a high-capacity foundation for a building, bridge, or other heavy structure. Nondisplacement piling typically involves drilling a hole down to a soil bearing layer and filling the shaft with reinforced concrete. Shoring is the process of providing temporary support for the sides of an excavation or trench to enable construction below ground level. Marine work typically involves construction of jetties and dock walls, as well as water and sewer intakes and outfalls.

Competition

Construction

The competition in the construction business is relatively localized to southern Ontario. In general, Canada's construction industry is fragmented, collectively dominated by a number of smaller operators. Although there are large players with nationwide coverage, smaller companies manage to survive in this competitive market due to the localized and specialized nature of their operations. Currently, there are about three foundation construction companies in Ontario who would be comparable technically to Jacoby. Among them, Deep Foundations Contractors Inc.

("Deep Foundations") and Anchor Shoring & Caissons Ltd. ("Anchor") are the two main competitors to Jacoby. They are both private companies. Deep Foundations has specialized in shoring for the Toronto condominium market. It is estimated to have some $35 million in annual sales. Anchor is a division of The Anchor Group, which was founded in 1968. It has over 35 years of construction experience in soil retention and engineered foundation systems. Anchor specializes in the design and installation of soil retention systems and caisson foundations.

Manufacturing

Jacoby is one of the largest manufacturers of foundation equipment in Canada. The Company's competitors in the manufacturing business can be categorized geographically: European, Chinese, and North American competitors. European manufacturers (e.g. Delmag GmbH & Co.) produce high quality and high price hammers, while about four competitors in China are providing smaller hammers at lower prices. The prices of Chinese hammers are only 60% of Jacoby's, while European products are up to three times as expensive as the Jacoby hammers. Although the quality of Chinese hammers is getting better, the marketplace perceives them to be of lower quality.

Historical Financial Review

Financial Results: Income Statement

Jacoby Construction income statement	2003	2004	2005	2006	CAGR (%)
Total revenue	14,625	17,182	29,060	27,545	
EBITDA (excluding operating leases)	778	2,724	4,484	5,355	62.0
Operating lease expenses	403	549	1,263	1,745	
EBITDA (excluding operating leases)	375	2,175	3,321	3,610	76.1
Amortization	787	750	824	815	
Net income	15	544	922	1,637	224.4

Source: Jacoby and Sons, Inc.

Jacoby, the combined company, has grown revenues by a CAGR of 23% per year since 2003.These results have been led by exceptional growth in Jacoby Manufacturing, achieving CAGR of 25% and Construction contributing greater than 16% to topline growth. Over the previous 4 years, Construction revenue contribution has averaged 68%, and in 2006, it followed that trend contributing 69%. In 2005, strong orders within the hammer sales area of Jacoby were due to a US

Army contract that was not repeated in 2006. The Construction division improved revenue by 11% in 2006, making up for the downturn in the Manufacturing division, leaving the combined company's revenue essentially flat year over year.

Historically, the Company has had an internal policy not to hold cash, but rather manage levels of bank advances. As a factor of their exceptional growth, the company has witnessed increased growth in its accounts receivable. In discussions with company representatives, they feel that write-offs are approximately 1% and it is an aspect of the business they monitor weekly.

The Company has maintained a consistent level on their revolver, and traditionally as the year progresses, it will pay down any increases it incurs. Similar to most construction companies, it has extended payables out to 75 days, but believe that with a recapitalized balance sheet and their current growth rate, it can lower that and take advantage of early payment discounts.

In addition to the above debt, the Company has a number of equipment financing agreements with Royal Bank and GE Capital totalling $4.4 million. This brings total debt to $12.7 million. As part of the use of proceeds, the Company intends to pay down the operating leases and move some of the equipment to the new Rental division.

A concern with the balance sheet of Jacoby is its ability to maintain a sufficient level of working capital. The business tends to have long cash conversion cycles, which limits the opportunities it can pursue.

Financial Forecasts and Growth Plan

Over the next 5 years, Jacoby plans to increase its revenues from the current level of $37 million to above $70 million per annum with a corresponding improvement in profitability. The Company intends to further enhance its unique synergy of construction and manufacturing as part of this growth program. Jacoby's core strategy is to leverage its specialization in foundation construction to become the industry leader, both domestically and internationally. The Company plans to expand its variety of technologies and services it offers, including manufacturing, leasing equipment, engineering services, and foundation testing.

Jacoby Construction Division

Jacoby aims to improve construction profitability by participating more in design-build team efforts, rather than acting solely as a subcontractor. Jacoby's reputation for technological innovation and successful recent projects, such as the Sir Adam Beck hydroelectric project in Niagara Falls, has increased the profile of the Company. Jacoby wants to capitalize on this by increasing its marketing efforts to the design-build industry.

Jacoby Equipment Leasing Company

After rapid growth in the rental business, Jacoby has decided to establish a separate equipment leasing company to capitalize on this growing market. A capital injection is required as the Company's current equipment rental fleet has limited inventory and often turns away larger customers/construction projects which usually have quick lead times and need equipment right away. Equipment rental is a high margin business and the creation of a leasing entity should increase manufacturing's gross margin. The leasing company will concentrate on larger projects with rental periods of 3 months or greater. In addition, the leasing company will expand into Europe, which is potentially a strong growth market for Jacoby.

Jacoby Engineering Services

The synergy of Jacoby's construction and manufacturing divisions places them in a unique position to assist other foundation contractors in planning and visualizing foundation construction projects. The Company is increasingly providing general contractors with detailed computer models of projects at the planning and bidding stages as well as throughout production. This allows Jacoby to recommend equipment and procedures, often leading to the sale or rental of equipment, and sometimes site supervision. Engineering Services is a growing and very high margin business for Jacoby. The Company plans to increase this business segment in the future, introducing a new type of consulting service to the foundation industry.

Consolidated Forecast

Jacoby's forecasted income statement includes the consolidation of the three operating divisions noted above and the inclusion of a targeted acquisition.

Jacoby consolidated forecast income statement (CDN$'000s)

Jones Construction Ltd.	CDN$000's	2006	2007e	2008e	2009e	2010e	2011e	CAGR (%)
Total revenue		37,357	41,469	53,290	25,658	64,017	69,568	1380.0
EBITDA (excluding operating leases)		5,355	5,631	8,321	9,804	11,057	12,326	21.6
Operating income		2,795	3,420	6,428	7,889	9,451	10,956	33.8
Net income		1,637	2,459	3,845	4,780	5,780	6,743	28.7

Source: Jacoby and Sons

Learning Notes

Now, Patrick Jacoby, the great grandson of the founder, needs to decide how to proceed with a $10 million financing. The key issues for him to contemplate are:

- What type of structure would be best for the company?
- How much ownership control (if any) has he prepared to relinquish to a new investment partner?
- How will this potential ownership shift affect the management succession and employee ownership plan Peter has for the firm?
- To whom should he look for the growth capital?
- Is the right management group in place to execute a growth plan?

Appendix 1: Industry Trends

It is a well documented fact that the state of infrastructure across the developed world is at a point where significant investment is needed to simply maintain the safety and functioning of the assets. Power generation facilities, roads, waste water treatment plants, bridges, and piers are under both physical and capacity strains beyond their design expectations. Governments have started to recognize this and have begun to commit funding, over a period of years, to the necessary investments.

In addition to the repair and maintenance needed on the existing infrastructure, new public infrastructure is being built in both the developed and developing world at an astonishing pace. For example, India is planning on spending roughly US$320 billion per annum on basic infrastructure by 2012. They estimate this figure will need to grow by 8% annually just to sustain the current rate of development in the country. Parallel to public spending, private organizations have significantly increased spending on large infrastructure assets, particularly in the resource and energy sectors.

Each of these large projects typically contains some element of specialty foundation work that Jacoby Foundation Solution either manufactures equipment for or directs contracts for.

Canadian Federal Government Spending

The federal government has also targeted the need to reinvest in transportation infrastructure with the announced total spending of $16.5 billion on infrastructure initiatives from 2006 to 2010. The Government's current infrastructure initiatives are noted below.

Canada's new federal infrastructure initiatives in 2006 (CDN$ million)

	2006–2007	2007–2008	2008–2009	2009–2010	Total
Funding for infrastructure initiatives					
Highways and border infrastructure fund	245	340	480	610	1,675
Canada's Pacific Gateway initiative	19	72	92	56	239
Canada's strategic infrastructure fund	–	181	429	570	1,180
Municipal rural infrastructure fund	200	332	450	550	1,532
Public transit capital trust	300	300	300	–	900
Existing infrastructure agreements	1,467	1,197	741	470	3,875
Funding for cities and communities					
Increase to 100% of the GST/HST rebate	625	650	685	720	2,680
Gas tax revenue funding	600	800	1,000	2,000	4,400
Total contributions	3,456	3,872	4,177	4,976	16,481

Source: Canadian Construction Association

In the 2007 federal budget, the Finance Minister also announced the following additions to infrastructure programs:

1. The Gas Tax Fund, which provides a share of federal gas tax revenues to municipalities to pay for municipal infrastructure, has been extended to 2013–2014 from its previous expiry date.
2. A new "Building Canada Fund" was created, which will provide $8.8 billion over 7 years to fund core infrastructure projects such as highways, cultural or recreational facilities, or water/sewer projects.
3. A new national fund for gateway and border crossings was announced with investments of $2.1 billion over 7 years.
4. Starting in 2007–2008, each province and territory will receive $25 million a year for 7 years for infrastructure projects.
5. An additional $1.25 billion was set aside for public–private partnership projects (PPP), whereby the federal government will fund 25% of eligible PPP projects.

Ontario Provincial Government Spending

Currently, the province of Ontario and its major municipalities are facing an infrastructure renewal crisis. It is estimated that 59% of Ontario's infrastructure is now more than 50 years old, and more than 70% of the useful life of public infrastructure has been used. The annual cost requirement for Ontario is estimated to be as high as $6–7 billion per year, up to a total for the province of $19 billion.

Private Sector Spending

Private investment is also participating in infrastructural development with pension funds undertaking a major shift in their investment policy towards infrastructure as an asset class necessary for the long-term pension requirements. Recent government initiatives and commitments have created a strong environment for private infrastructure investments and encouraged PPPs.

Public infrastructure assets are not the only ones in need of renewal. To support the expansion of the power generation industry (e.g., new nuclear plants) and the oil and gas sector (e.g., LNG gasification facilities, oil sands projects, etc.), there are a significant number of projects that will drive growth in this sector over the next decade.

Manufacturing Market

As the construction market in both Canada and the U.S. are expected to still be strong in the next 5 years, demand for construction equipment is expected to be high, keeping pace with the overall infrastructure spending. According to the Association of Equipment Manufacturers, overall construction equipment sales increased by 11.2% in US, 12.7% in Canada, and 10.9% worldwide in 2006. Through interviews with Jacoby's largest customers, they feel the demand for specialty foundation equipment will continue to grow at a significant pace moving forward. The global demand for heavy construction equipment is forecast to grow by about 5% annually from 2006 to 2009, reaching a US$110 billion value.

Appendix 2: Competition

Construction

The competition in the construction business is relatively localized to southern Ontario. In general, Canada's construction industry is fragmented, collectively dominated by a number of smaller operators. Although there are large players with nationwide coverage, smaller companies manage to survive in this competitive market due to the localized and specialized nature of their operations.

Currently, there are about 18 foundation construction companies in Ontario. Among them, Deep Foundations Contractors Inc. ("Deep Foundations") and Anchor Shoring & Caissons Ltd. ("Anchor") are the two main competitors to Jacoby. They are both private companies.

Deep Foundations has specialized in shoring for the Toronto condominium market. It is estimated to have some $35 million in annual sales. Anchor is a division of

The Anchor Group, which was founded in 1968. It has over 35 years of construction experience in soil retention and engineered foundation systems. Anchor specializes in the design and installation of soil retention systems and caisson foundations.

Manufacturing

Jacoby is the largest manufacturer of foundation equipment in Canada. The Company's competitors in the manufacturing business can be categorized geographically: European, Chinese, and North American competitors. European manufacturers (e.g. Delmag GmbH & Co.) produce high quality and high price hammers, while about four competitors in China are providing smaller hammers at lower prices. The prices of Chinese hammers are only two third of Jacoby's, while European products are up to three times as expensive as Jacoby's hammers. Although the quality of Chinese hammers is getting better, the marketplace perceives them to be of lower quality.

American Pile driving Equipment Inc., International Construction Equipment Inc., and Pileco, Inc. are three key players in the construction equipment manufacturing industry in North America.

American Piledriving Equipment Inc. ("APE") produces, distributes, and rents a variety of pile driving equipment including vibratory hammers. They do not rely on distributors, but rather rent and sell directly to contractors. With in-house machining and fabrication facilities, APE sells itself as having the flexibility to respond to job situations quickly. APE imports diesel hammers to the United States that are based upon 1930s German design and have been manufactured in Shanghai, China since 1997. APE's strong financing backing has allowed it to increase market share as the low price leader and currently has 35–40% of the market.

International Construction Equipment Inc. ("ICE") was traditionally a US-based manufacturer, but is increasingly importing equipment manufactured in China. The Company distributes pile driving, drilled shaft, and other deep foundation equipment, including diesel hammers. As the ICE diesel hammer is identical to the APE hammer, it had to match APE's low pricing strategy to maintain market share. ICE currently has the largest rental fleet in the industry.

Pileco, Inc. has specialized in distributing German-made diesel pile-driving equipment for more than 50 years. Recently purchased by German equipment manufacturer, Bauer Aktiengesellschaft in October 2005, Pileco distributes Bauer drill rigs, but also imports diesel hammers from China, which are also identical to the above offerings.

Jacoby's diesel hammer is differentiated from the above through higher technology, higher efficiency, and clean burning ability. Jacoby is also the only manufacturer that will customize its equipment to individual customer's requirements. The Company's primary constraint is the lack of available inventory.

Rental Business

The equipment rental market is growing dramatically and there are a large number of local equipment rentals, but only two main regional players: Sunbelt Rentals and Equipment Corporation of America.

Sunbelt Rentals, based in North Carolina, is the second largest equipment rental company in the US. It provides equipment rental solutions for the industrial, construction, and municipal markets, from a network of over 450 branches, including 100 outlets at Lowe's stores. Sunbelt's equipment fleet includes a range of general construction and industrial equipment and is further broadened by specialty businesses serving the pump, power, trench shoring, and scaffold markets. Sunbelt is a wholly owned subsidiary of Ashtead Group plc, a Toronto Stock Exchange traded company with a market capitalization of over US$1 billion. Sunbelt's FY2006 revenues were US$819 million with an operating profit of US$176 million.

Equipment Corporation of America ("ECA") is a distributor of new, used, and rental construction machinery for pile and foundation installation, hoisting and rigging, material handling, and other specialized, civil, mining, and marine construction projects. ECA is a third generation, privately owned, family business.

Both of the above companies offer Jacoby equipment for rent or sale.

Chapter 9
Case Seven: Mesbo Supermercats – A Traditional Catalan Firm Facing Its Succession

Introduction

This case was written by Alan Carsrud and Malin Brännback. It looks at the issues related to a large Catalan (Spanish) firm whose food industry is changing rapidly and who are faced with the issues of "cousin consortium" where there are family involved in the business and those whose only connection are dividend check. The firm and the individuals in it have been de-identified.

What Do We Do?

"I think we should sell now. You saw what happened with our rival Picker. They got more than $100 million and now they are retired and enjoying their lives, something we haven't done for years! We're always working ... and now we have to deal with all this succession stuff to boot. Who says our children aren't going to sell it in the future anyway?" Marcos Bo was venting to his brother Pablo who listened to him thoughtfully, as he had always done.

It took Pablo a long time but he had finally convinced his two brothers that they urgently needed to face their succession process since their retirement was no longer far off in the future (Jose and Marcos were in their 60s and Pablo was in his late 50s). Pablo was sure that no matter what the results, the process would allow them to get clarity on what could be done to better operate the business.

Hopefully, Pablo could get his brothers to also deal with several other things such as ownership rights and duties and succession plans. This latter issue was a subject that had been wholly avoided in the past. To facilitate the process, they agreed that they needed a consultant who was brought in during 1998. Pablo had hoped as he continued to listen to Marcos' complaints about the changing world of Barcelona.

A.L. Carsrud and M. Brännback, *Family Firms in Transition: Case Studies on Succession, Inheritance, and Governance*, SpringerBriefs in Business 3, DOI 10.1007/978-1-4614-1201-4_9, © Alan L. Carsrud and Malin Brännback, 2011

Catalonian Market

Catalonia is a region of Spain noted for its traditional small- and medium-sized companies where family-owned firms account for more than 75% of the total economic activity. Of the top ten supermarkets chains in Catalonia, four are family groups. However, two of them had recently been sold to multinationals and the sector was changing rapidly.

Until now, Barcelona, unlike the rest of Spain, was an area where the mega-stores had not really achieved much success. There were big malls outside the city, but the people living in the concentrated and urban areas of Barcelona continued shopping primarily in the inner-city. However, the Catalan groups were now facing the entrance of big competitors like Carrefour and Auchan, who were staking their claim primarily by acquisition.

Mesbo Supermercats

Mesbo Supermercats is a chain of 299 supermarkets operating in Catalonia, a region in the north of Spain. The group operates both owned and franchised supermarkets (The franchises represented 60% of the total). Mesbo employs 2,802 people and had sales and net profits of $382.5 million and $2.5 million, respectively, in 1999. As the largest supermarket chain in Catalonia (second largest in revenue), their slogan read "We are close to you."

The three Bo brothers, Jose, Marcos, and Pablo, had operated the business for 40 years, and in 1996 they created a Board of Directors with the brothers holding every seat; they also appointed a CEO and a management team, all of them young professionals that were relative newcomers to the company. The Bo family, however, did not have a Family Council. The always ate a long Friday lunch together and that seemed to suffice for discussing family matters, or at least Marcos and Jose thought so.

Brief History

Pablo, Marcos, and Jose Bo were three youngest of five siblings of a traditional agricultural Catalan family. Land and family wealth could never be divided, and following the ancient traditions, the first born male, their older brother Tomas, inherited all the family properties and remained in the family house. Their sister Lucia became a nun much to the happiness of their mother Isabel.

Because their brother would own the family farm, the three younger brothers decided they had to leave home as soon they finished high school. They ended up emigrating to the region's capital, Barcelona. Soon after arriving at Barcelona, in 1960, Jose and Marcos started working in a local market in central Barcelona. They earned enough that they could save one of their salaries and live off the other one.

One year later they bought their first small stall in the local market square. Pablo, the youngest, arrived a few years later and started working there with his brothers while going to college to get his economics degree. He had been lucky to be awarded a scholarship to university which paid his tuition.

Early Growth

From 1960 to 1980 the brothers acquired a total of 11 stalls. During this period their salaries fluctuated, consisting of what they took could reasonably take out of the business on a monthly basis. Luckily, the business was profitable and they were able to save and gather capital while at the same time gaining knowledge of the grocery business. That allowed them, in 1980, to open the first supermarket holding the name "Bo Aliment" (Bo food). One year later, the company's first warehouse was acquired to house the increasing inventory. The number of locations grew very quickly from there, reaching 55 in 1989.

This rapid growth was possible due to both the new supermarkets and their franchising system. The franchises started without much previous planning – long-time employees simply asked for support in setting up their own supermarkets. In response, the Bo's provided them with the merchandise, a unified brand name, and financial help. That was how Bo Aliment started operating in the distribution sector. The growth was fast and a bit unexpected. In fact, despite sales of $127 million in 1995, the brothers had installed little internal structure to the business.

Brotherly Responsibilities

From the beginning, the three brothers had played differentiated roles within the business. Jose, the eldest, was the outward front and handled much of the public relations and contract negotiation issues. He also played an important role in pushing for growth, mainly due to his aspirations for wealth, power, and social recognition. Marcos, the middle brother, was originally responsible for the purchasing, and he currently supervised the sales and marketing areas. Jose and Marcos shared much in common – they both led active social lives and were married to women that had worked for them as cashiers in the early market stalls.

Pablo, the youngest brother, had been in charge of all financial, legal, and personnel functions from the beginning. Even after new departments were created for these areas, he continued to supervise them. He was also the Chairman of the Board of Directors. The banks liked that he had a college degree and thus his brothers agreed he should be Chairman while Jose was more the defacto CMO and Marcos the COO. In his personal life, Pablo married a pharmacist he met at university. Together they aspired to build a stable family.

Although there had been some tension and conflict between the brothers, they had always overcome those events. They were fond of saying that "… three was a good number" since one of them, usually Pablo, could always balance the situation. However, Pablo wondered though how this balance could be extended to the following generation. None of his nephews or sons seemed to have his skills of keeping the family together.

Sharing Responsibilities and Expanding the Pie

As the years passed, the brothers filled managerial roles with people who had worked their way up through the business. The big shift came in 1995 when they moved to the current headquarter location and started creating a departmental structure. New, young professionals (with college degrees) were hired to help the three brothers run the business.

It was then that the current CEO of the company, Enric (36 years old), entered Mesbo after having worked at a major market chain based in Madrid. He understood from the start that this was a family business and he was part of professional management, not family.

On the acquisition front, a large family owned chain of Barcelona supermarkets was purchased in 1996 and several professionals from this group began to work for Mesbo. Not long afterwards, in 1997, a smaller acquisition took place of another family chain in Catalonia. Since then the group had consistently grown in units, sales, and profits (see Exhibit 1 for growth since 1990).

Three Families, Ten Cousins

The families (see Exhibit 2) had been deliberately kept apart from the process of building the business. The three brothers did not want to involve their wives, and later their children, in what they called "the problems and worries of the business." Jose and Marcos's wives stopped working for the business to take care of their homes while Pablo's wife ran her pharmacy and played the balancing role between her two sisters-in-law, getting the three families to gather at Christmas. Unfortunately, the two sisters-in-law did not get along with each other. Consequently, the cousins rarely saw one another and grew up, more or less, isolated from each other. This was not the same tight knit extended family Pablo remembered growing up in as a child in the country side.

Jose's Family

Jose had three children, Isabel, Jose Jr., and Jorge. Isabel, the oldest sibling (30 years old), had been studying law for years, but no one knew for sure whether she had finished her degree (although her father Jose always introduced her as a lawyer).

She had joined the company some years ago, doing administrative tasks and keeping a "flexible" schedule – coming in late and leaving early. She used to say that these were the advantages of having Bo as a surname. The previous summer, she married the head of the human resource department in the firm. Jose Jr., was 26 years old. He worked in the firm's main warehouse carrying merchandise, although he had previously done several small administrative jobs within the company. He had not gone to university but loved to play football and dreamed of being Real Madrid as a player. Finally, 20-year-old Jorge was more interested in partying and music than in his studies at university. He was a great disappointment to his father, Jose.

Marcos' Family

Marcos had four children, Sonia, Rosa, Marcos Jr., and Pedro. Rosa had been the first, together with Jose Jr., to join the company (both of them just after finishing high school). Rosa was 28 years old and worked in the purchasing department doing administrative tasks. Her twin sister Sonia was the first member of the second generation to obtain a college degree (Economics). After getting her degree, she worked for an auditing firm for several years before joining Mesbo. In Mesbo, she worked directly below the head of the financial department and had ambitions to eventually become the CFO. However, she felt undervalued and underpaid and was finding a lot of obstacles in her career.

For example, her salary was similar to her sister's and her cousins', whose responsibilities were far less important. Additionally, she received little of the support any other newly hired person would receive in Mesbo (presentation of the company, introduction to the different departments and people, etc.). Everyone at the firm, including her father and uncles simply assumed she already knew everything about the firm because she was a Bo. Marcos Jr. was 22 years old and had two years left to finish his university business degree. He expressed some interest in joining the family business sometime in the future. Pedro, the youngest, was 21 and had already joined (and left) Mesbo. He became a vegetarian and rejecting all sources of materialism decided he wanted to be a Hippie in California. He was a great disappointment to his father, Marcos.

Pablo's Family

Pablo had three children, Nina, Silvia, and Miguel. Nina was 25 years old and held dual degrees in pharmacy and business. After working for 2 years in a pharmaceutical laboratory, she went on to study for her MBA. She would finish soon and had to face a tough decision– choosing between attractive offers from several different companies around the world. From her perspective, she first wanted to work abroad and then possibly come back to the family business or her mother's pharmacy. Silvia was Pablo's second daughter. She was 22 years old and would be graduating with an MBA after spending some period abroad. She was looking for a foreign job currently, but would consider the possibility of joining the family business down the road. The last and youngest sibling was 19-year-old Miguel who was in his second year of a law program.

Pablo was very proud of all of his children as they were outstanding students and all possessed a wide range of talents in the arts and music. He learned, however, not to mention his children to his brothers as that would launch them off on monologues about the problems they were having with their children.

To the Rescue

The first time the family business consultant, Juan Martinez de Angel arrived in Mesbo's headquarters he found 16 people sitting around a conference table – the three brothers, their wives, and the ten cousins. He looked at their expectant expressions and felt as if they were looking to him to deliver a magic solution that would say "… the future for Mesbo is this … ." For their part, all the cousins had simply been told to go to the firm's offices for a meeting, but none of them knew exactly what they were supposed to be doing there and what they were going to talk about. Juan Martinez sensed immediately this was going "… to be one of those kind of meetings where skeletons come out of the closet."

The consultant could immediately sense the lack of connection between them all. He first got them to introduce themselves and also talk about what they knew or had experienced about Mesbo. That first meeting ended with a significant amount of finger-pointing and a large list of criticisms towards each other and the three Bo brothers. But at least the family got to talk about the business and their feelings and concerns towards it, something they had never done before together. Pablo was relieved that there was no shouting, but Marcos and Jose seemed threatened by the whole event.

Code of Silence

To date, secrecy had always dominated in the Bo family and Mesbo. In order to avoid problems, the three brothers did not want the wives involved at all in the company even though Jose and Marcos had married onetime employees. Jose, Marcos, and Pablo agreed to not to explain more than what was necessary to their spouses. And they followed the same rules with their children. Not wanting to worry their families, they would keep them in ignorance of anything related to the company. This situation went on up until the early 90s, when the three brothers started to be slightly, though not much, more open with their wives. The secrecy did not end with the fathers. Instead, it seemed to filter down to the individual families who appeared reluctant to share with one another.

After that first meeting, the consultant and his team held individual interviews with each member of the family and the different family branches. Through those interviews, the consultant realized that he was dealing with three distinct families with very different sets of values and priorities. He could also see that getting everyone to reach a consensus on one common list of values for the family and the firm would be a difficult thing to do. After the interviews, the family started holding periodic meetings to work on a family protocol, to establish succession plans, and to develop and understand the interests of the second generation.

Nonfamily Management

The nonfamily CEO and the rest of the management team were also interviewed by the consultant. They told him that they were completely in the dark about the future of the company and the succession of ownership and control. While they were all thankful for their rapid rises within Mesbo and recognized that, in another company, it might have taken them much longer to reach the same position. They still did not know whether the other siblings in the three branches of the family had plans to join the business. Their bigger concern was if they did join, how capable they were. They also told the consultant that they were excited by the idea of a defined strategic plan for the firm. They felt this could lead to a reduction of uncertainty about the future of the business. The consultant also recognized the inherent issues that existed for one of the management team members who had recently married a Bo. This young man sensed concern from others on the team that this fact would somehow change his loyalties, outlook, and position within the company.

Progress Made

Looking at the previous meeting's minutes, Pablo thought that things had really changed since they had started the whole process two years ago. He was a bit more relaxed, he could see the family was getting to some agreements, and that the protocol was starting to have a structure and some content (see Exhibit 3). Yet, he also wondered if they would end up having a very nicely written protocol and agreements that no one would care to fulfill. He did not worry as much about his children, but in his nephews and nieces he had less trust that they would carry out the agreement. Pablo also realized that his retirement as Chairman of the Board would probably still have to wait some years since he could not see any clear successor.

Expectations Expressed

As Pablo had expected, Rosa, Isabel, and Jose Jr. had made it clear to everyone that they did not expect any managerial or executive role in the firm. They did see the company more as a source of a guaranteed income than as a family legacy, should they work to continue. They specifically said that they considered themselves inadequate to take on such responsibilities. Still, they wanted equal salaries for everyone regardless of what they did in the firm and to be able to enjoy of some privileges of being family members (leaving job early, and extra paid vacation time). Pablo thought that was being a bit selfish on the part of some of his nephews and nieces.

Sonia, on the other hand, was absolutely dedicated to her work in Mesbo and everyone agreed. But her insecurity and excessive emotions did not make her the optimal family leader for the company. As for Pablo's children and Marcos Jr., they appeared to have at least the education that could make any of them good successors, but they still had to show their skills and capabilities through their experience in other companies. He also recognized that they might decide that it was better to be outside the Mesbo umbrella if they wanted to stand on their own two feet.

The possibility of having an outsider running the company was also in Pablo's mind. He felt that some seasoned professionals were needed to provide the company with fresh ideas. However, he wondered how they would be accepted by the family members already working in the company and by the existing Management. "Oh well!" Pablo thought, "let's go on with the protocol and meetings and see how things evolve but we will have to make a critical decision soon …. Mesbo and the Bo family need it …."

Exhibit 1

Year	1990	1991	1992	1993	1994	1995	1996	1997	1998	1999
Nr. supermarkets	55	61	71	79	84	103	242	255	270	299
Personnel	445	567	650	648	858	1,095	2,060	2,541	2,739	2,802
Turnover(in MM pts)	8,000	1,000	12,500	15,500	17,500	21,500	45,000	52,500	60,000	65,000

Exhibit 2

The three brothers and their siblings – *indicates those already working in the company.

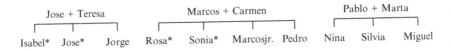

Exhibit 3

93

Exhibit 3

Results from the work done in the four meetings already held. In attendance were the three founders and their wives, their ten siblings, and Sonia's, Rosa's and Isabel's husbands. They defined the tasks and responsibilities and also some operating rules of the Family Council (new creation), of the Board of Directors and of the Management team (with CEO on command):

Family Council:

1. Propose and approve the members of the Board of Directors.
2. Approve the distribution of dividends.
3. Be informed by the Chairman of the Board of Directors about how the company is operating, in presence of the rest of the Board.
4. Establish the norms and requirements for the members of the family who want to join the business. Define the rules to determine the compensation of the family members and their spouses who work in the company.
5. Set the rights and duties derived from ownership.
6. Define the long-term strategy together with the Board of Directors (how we want the company to be operated, objectives, and goals).
7. Build the Family Protocol and review it periodically.
8. Supervise the Board of Directors. Approve their compensation and evaluate them.

The Family Council, after the initial period, is going to meet minimum once a year and maximum four times a year. The Family Council will have a chairman named by the family members and it is going to be one of the three founders. It will be a rotating position (period of time to be determined).

Board of Directors:

1. Maximum command in the company, ultimate responsibility to the Owners (Shareholders or Family Council).
2. Define the general strategy for the business (diversification, financing, etc).
3. Promote and review the strategic plan (3 years).
4. Define the strategy and the mid/long-term objectives that the Management will have to accomplish through the short-term objectives.
5. Approve and follow-up on the annual budget.
6. Choose and approve changes on the Management Team.
7. Approve the Organizational Structure of the company (new departments, increases or reductions of responsibilities, changes in the organization chart, etc.).

On the Board of Directors, there will be two representatives of each family branch (they can be family members or their spouses).

Management Team (CEO maximum responsibility):

1. Build the budget that (will be approved by Board of Directors).
2. Design the strategic plan.
3. Propose modifications of organization structure.
4. Propose to the Family Council the different positions of family members (both for the ones already working in the company and for the ones entering it).
5. Present financial statements and budget variances to the Board of Directors.
6. Responsible, in the last resort, for all the things that are not the specifically responsibility of the Family Council or the Board of Directors.

Conditions for family members to join the company:

1. Two years of working experience outside the family business.
2. They can enter in any of the three first (highest) levels of the actual organization chart.
3. A professional evaluation of the ten siblings will be done by an external Cabinet.
4. An external tutor will be named for each of the family members working in the company. The external tutor will design the development plan together with the corresponding managers or superiors.
5. The spouses will be considered as family members in all the situations and issues. There will be just one limitation – a couple cannot work in the same department and no subordination or dependency relation should exist between the two of them.
6. The compensation will be established according to the salary ranges of their position with a surplus or reduction of 10% (to be determined) because of being a family member.
7. CEO will place the family member in the position he/she considers most adequate for him/her; however, the candidate can express his/her preferences. If the family member disagrees, they can take the matter to the Board of Directors.
8. Family members should be ready to take on more responsibilities within the same job position because of belonging to the family.
9. Immediate superior should precisely define the outcomes and expectations for the family member(s) under his/her supervision.

The Family Council should follow up the performance of the different family members working in the company and propose promotions or corrective measures. It is important not to prevent their promotion and allow them to build their career path.

Exhibit 3

95

Learning Notes

1. Succession process: was it the right timing for the three Bo brothers to start planning their retirement? Was their previous attitude – secrecy – towards their families adequate, not wanting to involve them at all in the business and what consequences did this attitude have on their children and on the management team? How had they dealt with the siblings joining the business? Have they been trained correctly? Is equality a good solution to compensate them?

2. Selling was also one of the options for the future, should they have considered it more? Do you think they should go on with all the protocol and meetings before having it clear if any of the siblings is interested in continuing the business?

3. What effects had the quick growth on the firm? Did they achieve the correct structure or they should be hiring new professionals that brought to Mesbo new ideas and different perspectives?

4. They almost did not have employees leaving the company, on the contrary people develop their career within the company and most of the owners of the franchises were ex-employees. Is this a common fact in family business? Why?

5. The consultant noticed a high distance between the set of values of the different family branches. Is it going to be a critical issue? Would family therapy be recommendable?

6. There are a number of articles available that provide many important insights about the succession, that can be of great help for Mesbo in their process of planning the succession and implementing it. Could sharing these with the family members have helped in this process?

7. How should the family go about developing a mission, vision, and strategy? How does ownership converge with these processes? What is the Bo family currently doing to address these issues?

Chapter 10
Case Eight: JADDCO Laboratories, Inc. – Succession in a Technology-Based Family Firm

Robert Frank and Chris Tuffli provided the initial research for this case which was edited by Pablo Brezman and Colleen Robb. The case was written under the supervision of Alan L. Carsrud. This case which has been deidentified, deals with succession within a family-owned technology-based firm.

Introduction

"Blue – it is blue," Julia shouted. Julia Dwyer and her husband Lewis Davidoff were pregnant with their first child. It was a time for celebration. It was also a time for complication. Julia and Lewis had been talking about moving from the Bay Area back to the East Coast to be closer to both their families. That plan would now have to wait. Moving East would require changing doctors and healthcare plans. Since Julia suffered from an odd health condition that would require extensive monitoring during her pregnancy, it was a risk that any new plan would consider her ailment a preexisting condition and not cover some of the additional treatments needed. Had they moved before Julia became pregnant, this would not be an issue. It was too late for that now!

For several years, Julia's father John had secretly hoped that she would come home and work with him in the family business. Recently, his desire for this had become less secret. A lawyer by training, Julia had assisted her father when a former employee sued the company in early 1996. While Julia and John had worked well together, she was not certain she wanted to join the company full-time, despite the fact that her father's hints had become less and less subtle. The question facing Julia was should she ultimately return to the east coast and work with her father in the family's technology-based business.

A.L. Carsrud and M. Brännback, *Family Firms in Transition: Case Studies on Succession, Inheritance, and Governance*, SpringerBriefs in Business 3, DOI 10.1007/978-1-4614-1201-4_10, © Alan L. Carsrud and Malin Brännback, 2011

Evolution of Technology

For most of his life, John Dwyer had been an inventor trapped in the career of an optometrist specializing in low vision ailments. The major causes of low vision, or severe vision impairment, are age-related macular degeneration (central vision loss) and diabetic retinopathy (peripheral vision loss). Low vision can also result from glaucoma, inoperable cataracts, stroke, and multiple sclerosis. While very adept at diagnosing and treating such ocular ailments, what John really enjoyed was inventing. At the age of 54, he had his first major breakthrough.

John, a horrendous snorer, tried to design a device that would combine a noise sensor with a sleeping mask to vary the amount of light reaching the eyes. When the snoring tripped the sensor, the sleeping mask would let in more light, triggering a change in the sleeping cycle that would stop the snoring. It did not work, but John kept inventing. A colleague of John's suggested instead that the mechanism designed to vary the opacity of the sleep mask could be adapted for other purposes. This triggered another idea for John and eventually led to the development of the Bioptic Teleplexor. The Teleplexor is a mini-telescope mounted onto a regular pair of eyeglasses. The device covers only one lens and is used to assist those suffering from poor vision with spotting distant and not so distant objects. The first experiment was performed with one of John's favorite patients – he went with his next door neighbor's 7-year old son, David, to McDonald's where David was able to see the menu and order a happy meal for the first time.

By the time he turned 61, John had seen his last patient and was devoting all of his energy to JADDCO (John and Deidre Dwyer Company) Laboratories, Inc. Formed in 1982 and incorporated in 1992, JADDCO has annual revenue of $10 million. Ownership rests entirely within the Dwyer family as John and his wife Deidre each own 30%, while each of their four children own 10% (see Exhibit 1). John and Deidre have discussed transferring another 2% to each of the children, but have yet to act.

Low Vision Products

The Teleplexor put the company on the map. It has become a huge success in the low vision community and is responsible for over 35% of the company's revenue. John has been contemplating developing a consumer version of this product (the Teleplexor FX) that might appeal to concert and sporting event attendees; however, he is focused instead in developing new products.

The second major product JADDCO sells is the Laser Cane. The Laser Cane emits a laser beam to the front, left, and right of the bearer. This 3-directional beam makes use of a range-finding technique and a position-sensitive device (PSD) to identify distance to obstacles. The information is conveyed to the user of the cane through vibrations at three different frequency levels. The Laser Cane is responsible for nearly 35% of the company's annual revenues.

Problems in Product Development

John's current passion is the Low Vision Enhancement System (LVES). Few of his inventions have caused more grief or more excitement than the LVES. The best way to describe the LVES is as a set of real-life, virtual reality glasses. Miniature video cameras combined with an image-processing unit compile information from the wearer's surroundings and replicate these images in expanded format on the inside of the lenses. The image processor can be programmed to tailor the display to the visual capability of the wearer. The whole unit weighs a little over 2 lb. While it is expensive (retail around $7,000), it is the most effective mobility aid to sufferers of low vision.

The LVES has been in development for over 7 years. Because of the highly technical nature of the device, John contracted the project management to an engineer named Patrick MacArthur. Unfortunately, Pat's knowledge of miniaturization and software programming skills was inadequate and the device's development suffered. In 1993, after 3 years of launches, recalls, improvements, and relaunches, the LVES still was not marketable – personally torturing to John since such a great idea was not being properly developed. In addition, John and his accountants noticed that the LVES was eating into the company profits at a rapid rate. In one of the few moments when John did not enjoy being President of JADDCO, he fired Pat. It was the only time he has ever had to fire someone. He hoped this meant the end of trouble for JADDCO and the LVES. He wonders if he could have avoided making that decision.

To replace Pat, John hired a young, entrepreneurial engineer named Nicholas Benjamin, who brought in several other engineers with expertise in miniaturization and has managed to steer the LVES toward profitability. John now believes that the LVES is poised to be the firm's most profitable product. "It's amazing, but it works and the medical community loves it. By this fall we will have completed all recalls and upgrades. In addition, our reputation, which suffered during the dark period of development, is starting to improve. This thing should be making buckets of money by the end of the year." John had not looked at his accountants' reports, but the bottom line did seem to be improving.

Part of the improvement may also have come from postponing further work on some of John's crazier ideas. Several projects designed to make it possible for sufferers of low vision to drive automobiles (tentatively named the Auto Assist) were dropped. Julia, a lawyer, was thankful. She had considered such projects to be "torts waiting to happen." While things were improving, JADDCO hadn't heard the last from Pat.

The Lawsuit

In early 1996, Pat sued JADDCO for failure to pay royalties. During a business downturn, John and Pat had reached an agreement to temporarily suspend royalty payments. Like many of John's business arrangements, Pat and John had a verbal agreement with regard to the percentage of royalties to be paid on sales of the LVES (approximately $100,000/year for 30 years). Once business picked up and royalty payments recommenced, Pat sued to recover royalty payments foregone. John wonders what he should have done to avoid this situation?

The lawsuit couldn't have come at a worse time. While the LVES was lurching toward profitability, it wasn't there yet. Developmental losses were in the neighborhood of $2 million a year and John was skating on thin ice financially. The added strain of the lawsuit and risk of losing over $200,000 in royalty payments proved to be too much for him to face alone. "Up until the conflict with Pat everything about JADDCO had been fun. I was building things and playing with ideas and had a great team to work with on product development. Now I was dealing with the lawyers. I was completely out of the realm in which I was comfortable," he recalled. For legal advice on how to escape this predicament, John turned to his only daughter, Julia, for help. But should family be your lawyer was the question Julia had from the very start.

The Business and the Children

Like her three brothers, Dan, David, and Andy, Julia was a part owner of the company. Ownership, however, was where their involvement generally ended. John's eldest son David summed up the children's feelings, "It wasn't that we never considered joining the business. Even if it represented most of the inheritance we were to receive, we kind of figured it was Dad's hobby and he would sink or swim on his own."

David, like Julia, is a lawyer currently in private practice in New York. Prior to going to law school, he had received an advanced degree in biology paid for by his parents. His *juris doctor* was paid for by a scholarship for students intending to pursue a career with not-for-profit organizations. When he joined the New York firm, the scholarship had to be repaid. His parents covered the bill with money received from the success of JADDCO.

Over the years, his middle son Dan probably benefited most from JADDCO. He used his experience as a math teacher to start his own education software company, Knowlco, in 1990. Knowlco was a money pit for 5 years before turning its first profits in 1995. During that time, loans from JADDCO and his parents financed most of his R&D expenses. John had hoped that Dan (or Julia) might join and eventually run the business. Dan had his hands full with Knowlco, however, and would not consider giving that up to join JADDCO, even if Knowlco had yet to really make a lot of money for him.

The youngest son, Andrew, is a genius like his father, but without the practical side. He works as an economist for the Federal Reserve Board in Washington, DC. Since his undergraduate and graduate degrees were financed through scholarships, he is less indebted to his parents and JADDCO. John and Deidre did help him, however, with the down payment for his elegant Georgetown row house that he shares with his soon-to-be wife.

John and Deidre's only daughter, Julia, is a successful self-employed lawyer. Like her brother David, Julia's law school education was partially financed by her parents. Her interests lie in environmental activism and her most recent project involved saving Siberian Tigers. This is why when her father asked her to help him with his law suit she got worried. While she understands the issues, she is really an environmental lawyer, not an intellectual or contract law attorney. However, she has always found it difficult to say no to her father when he asked for her help.

Julia and the Business

When her father called about the lawsuit, she was in the midst of developing an environmental law education program in Russia. Becoming involved with JADDCO was a difficult decision, but she could not turn her back on her family, since she had always felt a little guilty about leaving the nest and fleeing to the West coast. She knew her father had always hoped she would join the business, but, beyond a sense of familial obligation, she had little interest in optical products. Julia was also concerned about her father personally. The hardships John had suffered at JADDCO over the past 2 years were catching up to him. Over the past 3 months, he had suffered several minor heart episodes and Julia was worried that if she did not relieve some of her father's burden, the next episode would not be so minor.

  Julia's attempts at resolving the lawsuit brought her a lot closer to her father and enabled her to understand him a lot better. She saw how much he really enjoyed the engineering and design aspects of the business, and how the stubborn father she remembered seemed much softer when she saw how he treated his employees. He was extremely loyal and appreciated all of his employees' efforts to help build the company. She also saw a social network that explained why he never seemed to do anything but work. John was completely immersed in product development and, for the most part, surrounded himself with people who felt the same way. On several occasions, he mentioned that he would trade an accountant for an engineer any time. "Thank the saints" she thought to herself, "he did not feel that way about lawyers given the number in the family."

  Julia also saw that her father's soft side sometimes undermined JADDCO's best interests. Late in 1995, Deidre discovered during a routine check of credit card reimbursements that the Head of Marketing and Sales was taking "excessive liberties" with his account. This employee is one of first hires John ever made. Even without the bogus reimbursements, he was one of the highest paid employees in the company. John refused to confront him over the issue. It turns out that this sort of naiveté in business matters is what saved John from losing his shirt in the lawsuit. As with many of his business arrangements, the royalty agreement between John and Pat had been a verbal agreement, which has a shorter statute of limitations than for written agreements. By the time Pat filed the lawsuit, the statute had expired. While the case has yet to be dismissed formally, legal action has been suspended and Pat recognized it would be futile to continue. But Julia wondered if her father, John, had learned his lesson from the lawsuit. She was not going to hold her breathe, for she knew her father too well at this point.

Everyone Gets Involved

One consequence of the lawsuit, however, was an increasing interest in the business by everyone in the family. Some of this was out of concern for the business and some of this was out of concern for John's health. Everyone wanted to avoid those economic downturns or physical problems. Even before the lawsuit, Julia had lobbied her brothers to take a more active role in overseeing the business. Countless conversation began with the phrase, "Couldn't you talk to Dad about...," but still her brothers adhered to the principle that this was their father's business to make or break. After the lawsuit, however, Julia began to see increased interest on the part of her brothers. On one of her trips home, Julia spoke to a friend over brunch at their favorite bar and grill which was literally a hole in the wall but with the best meatloaf in town. She told her best friend later "I don't know if it was my badgering or something else, but all of a sudden, David, Dan and Andy are thinking about the business and what it means to them. It's the strangest thing."

A Father's Reaction

Bemused was her father's initial reaction to the increased attention. Julia first saw that John was mildly intrigued by his family's new involvement in JADDCO. But, as time passed, his interest turned increasingly to irritation. All of a sudden he had board members challenging his authority and questioning his leadership. He was not sure which was worse, a lack of interest from the family in his business or too much interest. Despite the ownership structure, the company used to be solely his domain. After all, he had invented and sponsored the products responsible for the company's success. He was the one who had built the business from a good idea to a thriving venture with $10 million a year in revenues. Now his sons were asking him about the level of expenditures for R&D, and his daughter was asking about the direction the company was headed. What do they know about running a business? John was beginning to be very upset with children even if they were well intentioned.

His wife was an entirely different matter. She was pushing all the wrong buttons with her husband and pulled no punches in her comments. Even if she meant well in her questions and critiques, the logic was lost on John. His first and only reaction to her suggestions was that she "...had bad ideas." He would then go to his lab in the company and refuse to take his wife's calls. John has an enormous capacity for stubbornness and Deidre only fed the fire. Their relationship was becoming increasingly strained. Julia and her mother decided it was time to get some outside help.

Bring on the Consultant

To resolve the increasing differences of opinion, everyone agreed that an impartial view would be a good idea and decided to hire a consultant. Julia knew her father well enough to realize that while he had agreed to hire a consultant, he would not expend much energy finding one. Secretly, he hoped the whole thing would blow over like the lawsuit had. Julia, however, spoke with a friend of hers who had recently attended business school and got a list of names of good consultants to family-owned firms. One stood out. Michael (Mick) Richards had recently retired from Deloitte, the accounting and consulting firm. He seemed to have the right blend of technical and senior-level business experience that might appeal to her father.

John hired Mick, but had mixed feelings about him from the start. As Julia predicted, he respected Mick's experience and liked him personally, but John made it clear to anyone who would listen that he thought the money would be better spent on another engineer. To numerous people, he said "Sure there have been some rough spots in previous years, but it does not necessitate a *soup to nuts review* of *my* company. Things are turning around. The lawsuit is behind us and the LVES is positioned to be a profit generator. Next year looks like it will be very good for JADDCO. I like Mick, but it seems like we are wasting time and money since the company is in such good shape."

By mid-October, Mick's report was completed and distributed to the board members (for summary, see Exhibit 2). For the most part, the recommendations were not unexpected. Most recommendation concerned improving controls, primarily over financial systems. That recommendation did not bother John too much. He never spent much time on that anyway. What did bother him, however, was the lead recommendation. JADDCO should hire a business manager. What John heard in Mick's recommendation was "…replace John as the CEO."

The whole family knew that John would resist following this piece of advice. Under the pretense of discussing the entire consultant's report, Julia pushed for an official board meeting to coincide with the Christmas holiday. JADDCO board meetings were supposed to be held on an annual basis, but in practice were very rare. Julia had attended her first half-yearly meeting just that past summer to report on the progress of the lawsuit. While she was not certain how this overture would be received, she thought it was an opportunity to capitalize on the recent interest shown by the family. Somewhat to her surprise (and especially that of her father), everyone agreed to attend.

The Surprise

Although her father would probably disagree, from Julia's perspective the board meeting was a success (for agenda, see Exhibit 3). With the exception of hiring a business manager, John quickly agreed to implement all of Mick's recommendations.

On the main issue, there was a lot of discussion. Finally, after Deidre threatened to not sign an upcoming extension of JADDCO's line of credit, John said, "If that's what it takes to get you [Deidre] to sign the extension, then I will start the process, if everyone still thinks it's needed, before the May signing deadline."

The crowning moment of the meeting actually occurred outside of the preestablished agenda. None of the Dwyer men have much tolerance for long meetings. After 2½ h of discussion of financial data, employee manuals and expense reimbursements and, of course, the need for a business manager, Dan had just about reached his limit. His father had just concluded a rambling defense of his operational authority to run the business by saying, "I hope you all realize what is happening here. This business will never prosper if the board continues to try and micromanage my daily affairs."

Dan leapt at the opportunity to get something off his chest, responding, "I agree entirely. The purpose of a board is not to micromanage the company but to help focus it on longer-term, more broadly based issues. We ought to be developing a long-term plan and future meetings should be held solely to gauge whether or not the company is sticking to the plan. For instance, as part of a five or ten year plan, I think we really ought to be considering *exit strategy and succession planning*." The magic word succession had been spoken almost as an evil omen.

Julia and everyone else in the room sat in stunned silence. It was huge bombshell and no one was willing or prepared to talk about succession. Conversation quickly returned to whether or not to hire a business manager and the subject did not come up again before the end of the meeting. But John felt vulnerable deep inside and wondered why his children were seemingly turning against him. His wife he could understand and even forgive, but his children. What were they trying to do? Who could he trust in the family? He was starting to think "no one."

Post Board Meeting

Two months after the board meeting, things had not changed much. John had done as he promised and implemented some of the easier recommendations regarding the financial controls. So far, he has not lifted a finger toward hiring a business manager and the May deadline for the credit line renewal was quickly approaching. Julia and her mother sensed that her father was backtracking from the promise made at the December meeting. Revenues for the first 2 months seemed to vindicate his position, however, as sales had been better than the most optimistic projections. Several issues still weighed heavily on her mind. Her father was still dropping hints about her joining the business once she moved back East. Granted, the baby was still 3 months from being due and any move could not happen for another 6 months after that, but would she be willing to join the business? Did he want her to be the business manager? Was she to be the successor that her brother Dan insisted they consider at the board meeting?

Further, the whole notion of succession planning had plunged her back to feelings she experienced when her father first had heart problems. What would happen when he was gone? What would happen to the business after he died? JADDCO represented the bulk of her and her brothers' inheritance. While she was not concerned too much about money, Julia wanted to see something come out of the business. Closer to the present, JADDCO also represented most of her father and mother's retirement money as they have no other savings or investments other than the house. Her mother has some money saved up, but not a sufficient amount for them to retire on. John might very well work until he dies, but that does not ensure that the company will always be profitable, or her mother taken care of in her later years. Julia suspects that as her father gets older he might spend more money on kooky schemes such as the Auto Assist. "Can she really save her father from himself," she thought.

As the baby shifted positions inside her, Julia sat back on her porch and sighed. She was really looking forward to being a mother and was thankful for the gift of a child soon to be born. She was also just a little thankful for the timing of this gift as any cross-country move that would bring her closer to her family would have to wait. But what was she going to do was secondary in her mind after the baby.

Two Months Later

Despite his concession at the board meeting and Deidre's continued threat, John still resists hiring a business manager. He has instead brought back Mick Richards to conduct another review in light of the implementation of most of his previous recommendations. John holds out hope that the recent upturn in sales as well as his adherence to the rest of Mick's advice will demonstrate that a Chief Operating Officer (COO) is not needed. While all family members intend to hold John to his promise, they are waiting (again) for the consultant's report to give them some credibility. John's heart has been acting up again and all family members hope that a business manager will relieve some of the stress John faces as President. The family also hopes that a COO will focus John on succession planning, even if none of them believe that such a plan will be needed for at least another 5 years. The credit line is up for renewal in 2 months. The baby is due in 1 month.

Exhibit 1

JADDCO Laboratories, Inc.: Family, Ownership, Management Diagram

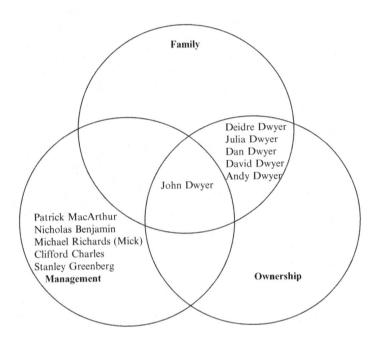

Exhibit 2

107

Exhibit 2

Summary of Consultant's Report

Report to JADDCO Laboratories, Inc.
October 14, 1996

Executive Summary

Generally, JADDCO is a vibrant, young company with dedicated and enthusiastic employees and creative products. The company has had a record of continuing growth, new products, and profitability. At the date of my review, JADDCO was reaching the limits of its banking line of credit. While the cash crunch may or may not be short lived, it has created an opportunity to see where weaknesses may exist and offer alternatives to strengthen the long-term viability of the company.

Recommendations

Hire Chief Operating Officer (COO). A COO with a strong background in marketing, manufacturing, and business would complement the strengths that the President brings in creativity and entrepreneurial skills. Such an individual would bring improvement to structure, planning and forecasting, inventory management and control, and financial reporting and controls. In addition, a COO would assist in implementing the more specific recommendations that follow.

Develop clear delegation of authority for supervising all segments of the company and provide a clear structure to enable day-to-day management functions to take place. Streamline existing structure that has 14 different individuals, including 11 different engineers, report directly to the President.

Establish a "Credit and Collections" function and provide the direction and time necessary to bring accounts receivable to a more current status.

Begin a budget and forecasting process that will take effect with calendar year 1997. Plan product upgrades to maximize the use of current inventory and avoid obsolescence of parts. Bring more focus to research and development plans.

Centralize the purchasing functions. Perform legal review of agreements with vendors.

Engage a firm of Certified Public Accountants to conduct a financial audit of the company's financial statements. Hire a cost accountant to develop the necessary procedures to perform product costing on an actual basis monthly.

Exhibit 3

Board Meeting Agenda (December 21, 1996)

I.   Review Financial Statements, third quarter fiscal 1996
II. Tax Issues, 1996
III. Tax Issues, 1997
IV. R&D Report
V.   Transfer of Stock Ownership
VI. Follow up on Michael Richard's Report

Attendees expected

    Board Members
       John Dwyer
       Deidre Dwyer
       Julia Dwyer
       David Dwyer
       Daniel Dwyer
       Andrew Dwyer

    Accountants

       Matilda Neubauer (agenda items I–IV)
       Clifford Charles

    Counsel

       Stanley Greenberg

    Matilda Neubauer is considered the JADDCO in-house accountant, although she is, in reality, little more than a very good bookkeeper. Clifford Charles, a family friend, has always reviewed the company's records. He has also prepared JADDCO's as well as the Dwyer family's tax returns for years. Stanley Greenberg is the JADDCO legal counsel. Julia Dwyer hired Greenberg to assist on the lawsuit. He remains on retainer to JADDCO.

Learning Notes

This case introduces many important family business issues which fall into the broad categories of succession planning, professionalizing the family firm, the role of the family board, and communications in the family business.

(continued)

Exhibit 3

109

Succession Planning

Succession is one of the issues critical to this case. As John Dwyer secretly hopes that one of his siblings with come back to run the JADDCO and Julia ponders the opportunity. There are two basic criteria for family member involvement: motivation and qualification. How does each of the Dwyer siblings stack up along these criteria?

Timing for sibling entrance: Dan and Julia present many windows of opportunity for entrance. Is there a window for Julia? What about Dan? There are three possible mode of entrance: full-time, part-time, advisory. Is one right for Julia? What might be the roles for the other family members? John Dwyer may work until he dies and will let succession happen after his death by someone else. John doesn't want to lose control over his life by hiring a business manager. Founders resist succession planning because it entails letting go their power to influence the day-to-day running of the business.

Western cultures have norms that prohibit open communication of issues like succession planning and financial matters. This contributes to John's "secret" desire to have Julia run the business with lack of any constructive communication. The founder needs to share learning, maybe to a business manager. The founder needs to cope with fears of death. The family needs to help the founder let go of the business by developing other interests. Creating a board that provides an independent perspective can help in the survival of the firm.

Resistance to succession planning may apply to this case. The owner's psychosocial bond and his need for control are obvious issues. The family firm represents "baby" as well as the "mistress" for the founder. It is John's source of energy and interest. It's difficult for entrepreneurs to give up what they have created. Other issues that can be raised are: (1) founder's lack of other interests; (2) avoidance of advice and consultation, (3) lack of open communication, and (4) heirs not motivated or qualified to take over. Siblings need to know that they have a choice to enter the family business. They need to be encouraged to figure out what they want to do and not be pressured to enter. John Dwyer does a good job of letting his siblings explore other interests, but then regresses by putting pressure on Julia to return to the family business.

Professionalizing the Family Firm

There are many reasons why a family firm should professionalize, two of which directly apply to JADDCO. The first is that sometimes the expertise and skills to run a business are lacking. In this case, John Dwyer's expertise lies in inventing and engineering products, not in the business and operational aspects of running a $10MM business. A professional manager could be used to run the day-to-day affairs of JADDCO, leaving John free to invent new vision products. A second reason hiring a professional manager is to prepare for succession planning. When and if John Dwyer decides to retire, a professional manager can be used to keep the family firm successful in order to preserve dividends or will make the firm more attractive if the firm is to be sold. There are three ways to integrate professional management into the family firm. John may want to bring in a professional family member. There may be one who is qualified, there may not. He may prefer to professionalize a nonfamily member, maybe a trusted engineer. He does not want to bring in outside professional management.

Role of the Family Board

The family board which is something that the Dwyer family struggled with at their first meeting. Nash also outlines ideas for the board's composition. JADDCO should compare adding outside directors as consultants vs. hiring an outside consultant. This may be a way to convince John to implement all the recommendations.

Family Communication

It is difficult to separate the personal role, family role, and equity role in the family business. Here are a few examples from the case: Julia and her siblings are concerned about their equity stake in the company. Julia becomes closer to her father after working with him on the lawsuit. Julia's guilt for not be a part of the company could stem from leaving the family and moving west. John and Deidre just do not get along. Any suggestions she makes with regard to the business are met with stubborn refusals that go way beyond just saying no.

Chapter 11
Case Nine: Frieda's Inc. – Successful Succession: Women Do It Right

Introduction

This case was researched and developed initially by Naomi Overton and Anthony Perez and was written under the direction of Alan Carsrud. This case has not been de-identified. It does represent a model for effectively transferring the ownership and leadership of a highly successful firm.

Announcing Succession

It was a typical warm July morning in 1986 in the downtown produce market area of Los Angeles. Frieda Caplan, President of what was then Frieda's Finest Produce Specialties, Inc. entered her eldest daughter's office as she usually did each day. In her normal matter-of-fact style she announced to Karen "We are making you president of the firm." Five years later, the company earned more profits in a month than it use to make in 1 year and had revenues in excess of $20 million.

Brief History

Frieda Caplan founded Frieda's Inc. in 1962 with her husband as a shareholder. Her husband, an active labor negotiator, encouraged his wife to do what she wanted to with regards to starting a business. At that time, she sold only California brown mushrooms, then an uncommon produce item. She soon gained a reputation in the regional produce industry for selling unusual food stuffs. She continued adding more fresh and packaged produce to her line. In fact, it was Frieda who introduced the now familiar kiwi fruit to North America. Even New Zealanders credit her with creating the world market for the then largely unknown Chinese Gooseberry.

A.L. Carsrud and M. Brännback, *Family Firms in Transition: Case Studies on Succession, Inheritance, and Governance*, SpringerBriefs in Business 3, DOI 10.1007/978-1-4614-1201-4_11, © Alan L. Carsrud and Malin Brännback, 2011

The now familiar "Frieda of California" purpleheart logo began to appear in most supermarket produce sections in California and the western United States on the labels of many unusual items such as purple potatoes, passion fruit, and spaghetti squash. In 1991, the company's name changed to just "Frieda's." It has been considered the leading marketer and distributor of exotic fruits and vegetables in the United States for many years. By 1996, it handled more than 400 different items. Once a product is carried by general distributors, Frieda's may drop it from their line to develop the markets for newer produce with higher margins. The company was the first wholesale produce company in the United States to be founded, owned, and operated by women.

Produce Industry

The fresh produce industry in the mid 1990s was made up of multiple suppliers, distributors, and retailers. Suppliers are growers of fruits and vegetables located not only in California and neighboring Mexico, but also around the world. Distributors deal primarily on a regional basis, supplying retailers with common varieties of produce. Retailers are typically grocery and specialty food stores. The industry is characterized by personal relationships established by literally an "old-boy network" of distributors, suppliers, and retailers.

Growth in the industry in the mid-1990s was strong. Since the early 1980s, American consumers have emphasized eating lighter and more nutritious food including more fresh fruits and vegetables. Swelling interest in organic and gourmet foods has also spurred growth in the use of specialty produce. Due to the relatively low sales volume of such "niche" produce, major distributors have historically chosen not to carry them. This opened the door for only a handful of companies to take advantage of this market niche. The largest produce distributors in the United States are Sunkist and Dole. The largest specialty distributors are Frieda's and Melissa's.

Business Situation

Frieda's remains distinctive in the specialty produce industry because it has created most of the markets for specialty produce, not just kiwi fruit. The firm enjoys considerable respect by competitors in the industry and has a dominant share of the specialty produce markets. It is the company that retailers turned to when they needed new exotic produce.

The primary competitor is Melissa's which was founded in 1984 by a former employee of Frieda's. This firm remains much smaller than Frieda's. Other competitors include Merex and J.R. Brooks which publicly have announced they aspire to be the Frieda's of their respective geographical regions. Yet, to many it is Frieda's that has created new markets by introducing new produce products. Certainly competitors have had a somewhat easier job in that they merely followed Frieda's lead.

This orientation as a marketing-driven distributor has required that Frieda's expend a great deal of effort in building brand equity in the Frieda's name. First the founder Frieda, and now her daughter Karen, spend a great deal of time doing media interviews, undertaking speaking engagements at a wide variety of public forums. Unlike most distributors, Frieda's has a full-time publicist on staff.

Key Players

Frieda Caplan. In 1991, Frieda became Chairman of the Board at Frieda's. She entered the produce business inadvertently in 1956, the year after Karen's birth by accepting a position with her husband's aunt and uncle who had a firm in the Los Angeles produce market. A few years later, with a $10,000 loan from her father, Frieda began her own company.

During her college years at UCLA, Frieda was active in school politics. In various positions she promoted cases and candidates and created a spotlight for others. This demonstrated her tendency in later years to promote and nurture others. In 1951 she married Alfred Caplan, a well known labor organizer who eventually operated his business out of the family home. Early on, he supported women's rights, partially because he believed that discrimination against any group degraded the quality of a work environment. He actively encouraged Frieda to start her firm. Over the years, Frieda found she enjoyed being involved in the hands-on operations of the firm, especially working with growers to discover unusual produce items and bringing them to market. While clearly an entrepreneur, she did not enjoy the day-to-day administration of the business.

Frieda and Alfred have two daughters, Karen, born in 1955, and Jackie, born in 1958. Frieda's long work hours in the produce market required that she and Al have help in bringing up Karen and Jackie as well as help in house cleaning. Frieda's work hours also led Karen to take up cooking the family meals at a young age. Despite working long hours, Frieda's daughters felt that she was always available to them when they needed her most.

Karen Caplan. Karen began working with the mother in the produce market at the age of 10. She formally joined the firm in 1997 after graduating with a degree in Agricultural Economics and Business Management from the University of California, Davis. However, she had not always planned to work for Frieda's. During her sophomore year at Mills College in Oakland, Richard Hernandez, one of the top employees at the firm visited Karen and suggested she consider joining her mother in the business when she graduated. Within hours of that meeting, Karen decided her best career opportunities existed at Frieda's. The following year she transferred to UC-Davis, known for its agricultural programs. She focused her studies on preparing to join the family firm.

When Karen finally joined the firm, there were only 20 employees and was located in the Los Angeles Produce Market. For the first year, Freida assigned Karen to perform tasks and projects that required immediate attention. This allowed Karen to work in all parts of the firm. Looking back, Karen views one of her initial achievements as having built a structured sales department. Karen became director of national sales and supervised the sales staff. She also managed Produce Dock, Inc., a wholly owned subsidiary of Frieda's that was responsible for packaging and shipping product for Frieda's. At this time she met Ray Jackson, one of the first employees at Produce Dock. In 1984 Karen married Ray and had their first child, Alexandra Nicole in 1989. Before Karen became President of the firm, she was Vice President and General Manager with responsibility over all sales and marketing efforts.

Ray Jackson. Ray joined Frieda's in early 1977. Early in his employment, Frieda pulled him aside and told him "you have a future in this company, young man." Frieda rarely did that and Ray soon became a supervisor and eventually the company's Operations Manager. Though titles and responsibility continued to come his way, he did not particularly wish for them. Ray valued working in the warehouse most. He had no real desire to hold positions elsewhere in the company, nor did he want to be involved in running and owning Frieda's. He reported directly to Karen since she was in charge of Produce Dock, Inc. in 1978.

Jackie Caplan Wiggins. Frieda's second daughter, Jackie, started working in the firm when she was a little girl, doing odd jobs like putting out mailings. She officially joined the firm in 1983. She is now Vice-President and spends 75% of her time selling to the company's key accounts.

After graduating from college she had two goals: travel and ski. She attended UC-Santa Cruz, UC-Berkeley, and graduated with honors from San Diego State University. She returned to Frieda's briefly after college before embarking on her travels. She spent 3 years traveling and working at ski resorts. Jackie has competed in several triathlons.

One day in 1983 she called her sister and asked "can I come to work for Frieda's again?" By 1991 Jackie was working in sales and reported directly to her sister and indirectly to the sales manager. Jackie had declined an opportunity to be the sales manager in the past because she enjoyed working with clients directly. Jackie also believed she could contribute most to the firm if she remained in sales. Any performance reviews she received came from her sister and not the sales manager.

Jackie is now married to Doug Wiggins, who owns a small produce firm and is a customer of Frieda. She met him when she worked on this account. While Jackie will sometimes work with her husband on his business, her first loyalty is to Frieda's.

Estate and Succession Planning

Estate planning preceded the succession planning at Frieda's. In the late 1970s Frieda and Alfred set up their wills to give 75% of the business to Karen and the remaining 25% to Jackie. The assets received by their half brother, a son by Alfred's first marriage, would not be connected to the business. At the time Karen was the only child involved with the firm and the majority share would give her controlling interest in the business. As Jackie became involved in the business, the ownership changed but the management did not. In 1989, the senior Caplans felt, as did Karen, that the 75–25% split was unfair. At Karen's recommendation, they realigned their wills and gave 55% of the firm to Karen and the remaining 45% to Jackie.

The potential for growth of the business was clear by the mid-1980s and it became apparent to Frieda that a change in management was be needed. Karen was instrumental in constructing the growth plans for the company's future. Frieda, not an administrator by nature, felt she was not the one to carry out this growth plan. She knew Karen's strengths would serve the firm well as the new president.

Meanwhile, the firm was about to have its 25th anniversary and Karen was about to turn 30. Frieda made it her mission to turn the presidency over to Karen in time for these two milestones. The major obstacle to the success was Alfred, who owned 50% of the company. Although confident of Karen's abilities, he believed Frieda's was Frieda Caplan and that the company would suffer without its founder at the helm. Frieda eventually convinced Alfred that Karen should be president, just weeks before the firm's anniversary and Karen's birthday.

Succession and Estate Implementation

Karen's transition to the role of president was rapid, and in her opinion, smooth. After Karen was told she would become president, she assumed the transition would take several months. The following Tuesday, however, Frieda announced the change to all of the employees, issued a press release, and left with Alfred on her first 2 week vacation in 24 years. Clearly Frieda intended to send the message to employees, clients, and the industry that Karen was taking full charge of the business. In late 1990, the Caplans sold the business to Karen and Jackie. They gave each child the maximum tax-free lifetime gift (at the time) of the business. The remainder of the sales price was carried in a note to the parents to be paid back out of the firm's case flow. As of November of 1990 Karen and Jackie had full ownership of the business.

Family Relationships in 1991

Karen and Frieda. Neither Karen nor her mother could pinpoint the events that led to the succession decision. Frieda felt that Karen was doing job and the time had come for her to take over. Krieda said she was relieved when Karen took over responsibility for the business. Karen knew she would make the transition work. She described her management style as "benevolent dictator." Her management motto was that she encouraged everyone to get involved in making decisions, but she still reserved the right to make the final decision.

After Karen became president, she had the authority to override decisions that Frieda made. She always knew Frieda would remain involved in the business. The most difficult part of the transition, according to Ray and Karen, was getting Frieda to relinquish control of day-to-day operations. In addition, Frieda and Karen had to direct both employees and the industry to ask Karen questions, rather than asking Frieda. This transition element took years to accomplish. Frieda said she was happier doing new product development rather than in have the strategic and administrative responsibilities for the business. Both felt they worked well together because they had complimentary skills.

Karen and Jackie. Over time Jackie became increasingly involved in the strategic decisions of the business. Jackie felt satisfied that Karen was the president and had the overall responsibility of running the firm. Jackie felt Karen was more concerned about status and titles than she does. Jackie admits she prefers a lifestyle that allows her more freedom outside work to pursue other personal interests. In addition, Karen preferred making decisions slowly and utilized what she called a "ready-aim-aim-fire" approach. In contrast, both Jackie and her mother preferred a quick, action-oriented decision making style. Furthermore, Jackie and Frieda were more project-oriented than Karen, who maintained a strategic planning perspective.

As with other family relationships in the business, the sisters were very professional while on the job. When Karen was away, Jackie would handle her sister's accounts. The two shared the largest accounts in the firm.

When Jackie first began to work at Frieda's she had some conflicts with Karen. Jackie felt that Karen assumed an "older sister" management style that caused Jackie to react like a "little sister." To outgrow this traditional relationship Jackie discussed this issue with Frieda. The result was that Frieda, Karen, and Jackie would meet periodically to find a better way of working together. Jackie worked with Ray often and said that their relationship functioned well. However, she made it clear that she would not want to work with her husband in his business other than when he had special projects. Overall, Jackie felt good about the transition at the firm and stated that her talents and ambitions complemented Karen's. Jackie added she believed her personality more closely resembled that of her mother.

Karen and Ray. Since Karen took charge of Produce Dock, Inc. in 1978 she has supervised Ray. Initially, Karen sought his advice about the business because of his many years of experience at the firm. As time went, Karen and Ray developed a friendship that later turned into love. The two were married in 1984, 2 years before Karen became president. Ray was supportive of his wife's interest in becoming president and he felt she could run the business skillfully. When asked about successors for the firm, both Karen and Ray indicated that Ray had no interest in running the firm. Overall Ray is satisfied with both Karen's role and his own in the firm. Although he has been invited to attend board meetings (consisting of Frieda, Alfred, Karen and Jackie) he has declined to attend.

Ray and Karen indicated that if the business became too large or too structured, Ray would have no problem leaving Frieda's. He added, his personal relationship has not affected his business decision, but that he just prefers a small firm. In addition, he has strong feelings about not discussing business at home. As Ray works different hours than does Karen (he is at work very early in the morning and comes home earlier than she does), he can spend more time with their 18-month old daughter while she is awake. This also enables Karen to have more time at work.

Karen and Alfred. According to both Karen and Ray, Karen and her mother needed to convince Alfred that Karen could handle the president's role. After succession occurred, Alfred started calling quarterly board meetings. Previously these were held rarely if at all. Though Alfred never had a hands-on role in the firm, he was accustomed to being kept up-to-date by his wife and providing strategic advice when needed. The transition caused him to implement a formal mechanism for keeping track of the firm, which he still partially owned at that point. When asked about their father's attitude toward the business when she was growing up, Jackie felt her father might have resented his wife's success somewhat.

Post-Succession

There have been several noticeable changes in the specialty produce industry and in the management at Frieda's since succession occurred. The company has enjoyed steady growth in sales and profits, growing from $11 million in revenues to $21 million. Several large produce and food companies have offered to acquire Frieda's, but the sisters have declined since they believe this would ruin the specialty image of Frieda's. Karen has attained industry wide recognition by being the first female president of the Fresh Produce Council. She is very active in a wide range of speaking engagements. Frieda and Karen have made a conscious effort to have Karen replace Frieda in the limelight. However, according to Jackie, some industry analysts still mistakenly believe that Frieda is still running the business.

Karen has made some internal changes at the firm. She created a management team to oversee new functional areas that arose while growing the firm. Karen did not see her transition to president as difficult as she was already performing many of these tasks as Senior Vice President. Karen's view of her mother's transition was different. Frieda's transition took longer as she was use to overseeing the details of the business, including reviewing every invoice sent out. However, now Frieda says she is relieved she no longer has responsibility for running the business. She is enjoying her focus on new products and market development, which has always been her first love.

The Future

Several questions about the future of Frieda's remain unanswered. What were the factors that led to this apparently successful transition? Can these factors be reproduced in the next generation? Karen has considered the possibilities for the future. One option is to continue to run the firm despite offers from major consumer brand conglomerates. The question remains whether the firm could be acquired, while growing rapidly, and still maintain its specialty produce niche position. Rapid growth, whether the firm is owned by the sisters or owned by a larger firm, have implications for Ray's position as well.

Karen is aware that her own daughter might someday have an interest in the firm, but feels that since Alexandra is only 18 months old it is too far in the future to make those plans. She also wonders whether her and her daughter's personalities will compliment each other as was the case with her and her mother. Ray's hope for their daughter is that she would join the business by her own choice. There is also the issue of Jackie's child and succession. With her sister in the middle of a pregnancy, Karen thought again it was too early to consider this. Though Karen prided herself on her ability to look into the future, she said the had learned from Ray not to look "too far into the future."

Another issue was Jackie's role going forward in the business. Both Karen and Jackie emphasized that Karen was in charge and both liked things that way. What would happen if Jackie ever wanted to play a more strategic and management role in the firm? If so, what would have to change? Jackie was becoming involved in new ways, by interviewing new job candidates who would work in other parts of the firm. Given that no formal plans have been made for possible succession, only time could answer these questions.

Learning Notes

Overall. Was this success story a fluke? What factors allowed for such a smooth transition and can this be repeated? What practical lessons, if any, can be applied to other family businesses planning for succession?

Letting go. Both Frieda and Alfred dealt wit the issues of succession and inheritance early on. They paid close attention to the tax implications as well as managerial and control issues. This contrasts with many entrepreneurs who hold on to their firm for as long as possible and see succession planning as loss of identity or death. A key factor in this case is that Frieda and Alfred did not keep ownership, and thus relinquished all formal control of the business. Furthermore, Karen was designated the clear, majority owner, and leader. The woman's different operational styles could also be key factors in this case. Karen's training and decision style and long-term focus were different from those of her mother or sister. Karen planned her entrance into the firm by studying a relevant subject in college and taking the initiative to focus her college work on the family business concerns. The fact she worked in nearly every area of the firm also trained her to take over the leadership role. Did Frieda really let go of the firm?

Succession timing. What triggered Frieda to hand over the reins when she did? Frieda and Jackie claim it was due to the combination of Karen's desire to become president by age 30 and the timing of the 25th anniversary of the firm, yet Karen does not recall a desire to be president by age 30.

(continued)

Complementary roles and goals. The nonconflicting roles and goals for each of the family members was clearly an essential element of this transition and its success. Jackie, like her mother, is project oriented, rather than strategically focused like Karen, her father, or a typical manager. Jackie chose selling rather than being a sales manager. Ray too likes the operations side of the business.

Husband and wife dynamics. This case also illustrates three examples of career dynamics. Alfred was very supportive of women and equal rights, and his choice to work from home made rearing Karen and Jackie easier for both he and Frieda. Similarly, Ray believes in Karen's abilities and helped her work toward being president of the firm. He works different hours than Karen and so he contributes to the care of his daughter as well. Karen and Ray interact professionally at work and separate their business and personal lives. The fact that they worked together for years prior to marrying may have contributed to this. Jackie and her husband, Doug, seem to know and accept their respective roles. Neither have a desire for Doug to join Frieda's

Gender factor. Would the succession seen in Frieda's have done as smoothly if Frieda had been a "Fred?" What if Karen had been a: Ken?" What if Jackie had been an only son "Jack?" Karen commented that she saw the succession as a fluke of nature and that its success stemmed from the fact all three were women and nurturers. Karen continued by saying that no male egos were involved to complicate matters. Is this true even with Alfred in the picture? What might be the effect of the fact that this was a female owned and managed firm in a male-dominated industry?

About the Authors

Malin Brännback, D.Sc. is Chair of International Business at Åbo Akademi University where she received her doctoral degree in management science in 1996. She also holds a B.Sc. in pharmacy. Prior to her return to Åbo Akademi University in 2003, she served as an Associate Professor in Information Systems at University of Turku, and Professor of Marketing at Turku School of Economics. She is Docent at the Turku School of Economics where she taught prior to returning to Åbo and she is Docent at the Swedish School of Economics and Business Administration in Stockholm. She has held a variety of teaching and research positions in such fields as Information Systems, International Marketing, Strategic Management, and Pharmacy. She has published widely on entrepreneurship, biotechnology business, and knowledge management. Her current research interests are in entrepreneurial intentionality, entrepreneurial cognition and entrepreneurial growth, and performance in technology entrepreneurship, especially within the field of life sciences.

Alan L. Carsrud, Ph.D., Ec.D (h.c.) is Professor of Entrepreneurship & Strategy and holds the Loretta Rogers Chair in Entrepreneurship in the Ted Rogers School of Management at Ryerson University in Toronto, Canada. His BA degree from Texas Christian University was in psychology, sociology, history, and anthropology. He received his doctoral degree in social psychology from the University of New Hampshire in 1974 and did postdoctoral work in applied psychology at the University of Texas at Austin. He holds an honorary doctorate in economics from Åbo Akademi University in Finland. Prior to his appointment at Ryerson he was the Professor of Industrial and Systems Engineering, Clinical Professor of Management, and Executive Director of the Eugenio Pino and Family Global Entrepreneurship Center at Florida International University, Miami, FL. He previously has served on the graduate entrepreneurship faculty of the Anderson Graduate School of Management of the University of California, Los Angeles, CA; the Australian Graduate School of Management, Bond University, Gold Coast, QLD, Australia; the University of Southern California, Los Angeles, CA; Pepperdine University, Malibu, CA; and the University of Texas at Austin, Austin, TX. He has published over 160 articles, chapters, and books in entrepreneurship, family business, biotechnology, industrial and applied psychology, social psychology, and clinical psychology.

Made in the USA
Monee, IL
15 September 2022

14043908R00077